FREEDOM AND PARTITION

FREEDOM AND PARTITION

Momentous Events of 14–17 August 1947 in India and Pakistan

TAN TAI YONG
GYANESH KUDAISYA

PRIMUS BOOKS
An imprint of Ratna Sagar P. Ltd.
Virat Bhavan
Mukherjee Nagar Commercial Complex
Delhi 110 009

Offices at CHENNAI LUCKNOW
AGRA AHMEDABAD
BENGALURU COIMBATORE DEHRADUN GUWAHATI HYDERABAD
JAIPUR JALANDHAR KANPUR KOCHI KOLKATA MADURAI MUMBAI
PATNA RANCHI VARANASI

ISBN: 978-93-5687-068-0 (Paperback)
ISBN: 9978-93-5852-022-4 (PoD)

Published by Primus Books

Lasertypeset by Sai Graphic Design
Arakashan Road, Paharganj, New Delhi 110 055

'Independence Day ceremonies deserve serious scholarly attention and should be set in a longer historical time-frame and broader geographical perspective. . . . The ceremonies marking India's independence in 1947 provided a prototype and model.'

—DAVID CANNADINE, Dodge Professor of History, Princeton University

'Partition is difficult to forget but dangerous to remember.'

—KRISHNA SOBTI, Hindi litterateur

'We are engaged in a war of narratives, incompatible versions of reality, and need to learn how to fight it.'

—SALMAN RUSHDIE, PEN America's 2022 Emergency Writers Congress

Contents

List of Abbreviations ix

List of Illustrations xi

Acknowledgements xv

Introduction 1

14–17 August 1947 and the Celebration of Independence 24

Epilogue 154

Glossary 181

Bibliography 185

Index 199

Abbreviations

ADC	aide-de-camp
AICC	All India Congress Committee
BBC	British Broadcasting Corporation
BJP	Bharatiya Janata Party
CA	Constituent Assembly
CC	Congress Committee
CHT	Chittagong Hill Tracts
CRO	Commonwealth Relations Office
DK	Dravida Kazagham
DMC	Delhi Municipal Corporation
HE	His Excellency
HM	His Majesty
HMSO	His Majesty's Stationary Office
IB	Intelligence Bureau
ICHR	Indian Council of Historical Research
ICS	Indian Civil Service
IGNCA	Indira Gandhi National Centre for the Arts
JNSW	Jawaharlal Nehru Selected Works
KPMP	Kolkata Partition Museum Project
MEA	Ministry of External Affairs
NWFP	North Western Frontier Province

PTI	Press Trust of India
RSS	Rashtriya Swayamsevak Sangh
UK	United Kingdom
UPPCC	United Provinces Provincial Congress Committee

Illustrations

Plate 1:	Jinnah's arrival at Karachi Airport, 7 August 1947	58
Plate 2:	Mountbatten at the Constituent Assembly of Pakistan session in Karachi, 14 August 1947	67
Plate 3:	Jinnah addressing the Constituent Assembly, 14 August 1947	68
Plate 4:	Fatima and Mohammad Ali Jinnah and Louis and Edwina Mountbatten in Karachi	69
Plate 5:	Mountbatten and Jinnah at the Constituent Assembly	70
Plate 6:	Jinnah taking the oath as Governor General from Justice Mian Sir Abdul Rashid	72
Plate 7:	Jinnah after taking oath as Governor General of Pakistan	73
Plate 8:	Liaquat Ali Khan after swearing in as Prime Minister	73
Plate 9:	Jinnah with Liaquat Ali Khan and his Cabinet	74

Plate 10: Fatima and M.A. Jinnah arriving at Karachi Club on the evening of 14 August 1947 75
Plate 11: 'Tilak' being put on Jawaharlal Nehru after a Hindu *havan* ceremony at Rajendra Prasad's residence on the night of 14 August 1947 83
Plate 12: Rajendra Prasad, President of the Constituent Assembly, congratulating Mountbatten on his appointment to the Governor Generalship of the Dominion of India from 14 August 1947 84
Plate 13: Singing of nationalist songs during the midnight session on 14–15 August 1947 85
Plate 14: Scene from the midnight session. Front row: Amu Swaminathan and G.V. Mavalankar. Back row: Mohanlal Saksena and Pattabhi Sitaramayya 86
Plate 15: Sarvepalli Radhakrishnan addressing the midnight session before the 'Tryst with Destiny' speech 86
Plate 16: Dr Rajendra Prasad presiding over the proceedings of the midnight session 87
Plate 17: Oath of allegiance being taken in the Constituent Assembly. Front row: Sardar Baldev Singh (left) and Jawaharlal Nehru (right) 87

Plate 18: Jawaharlal Nehru delivering his historic 'Tryst with Destiny' speech 88
Plate 19: Swearing-in ceremony in the Durbar Hall of the Viceroy's Palace on the morning of 15 August 1947 93
Plate 20: Nehru and the Mountbattens at Central Vista on 15 August 1947 94
Plate 21: Crowd scenes outside Constituent Assembly in the morning of 15 August 1947 96
Plate 22: A photograph of crowd scenes at the inter-services rally at India Gate on the evening of 15 August 1947 97
Plate 23: Women and children at India Gate on the evening of 15 August 1947 97
Plate 24: The Mountbattens, Pamela, Louis and Edwina, watching a juggler's trick in the midst of celebrations at Roshanara Gardens in north Delhi on 15 August 1947 98
Plate 25: Children getting sweets in Delhi 99
Plate 26: Seen at the Red Fort on the morning of 16 August 1947 100
Plate 27: Decorations and crowds in Chandni Chowk, Delhi 101
Plate 28: A portrait of Netaji Subhas Chandra Bose with the banner 'Lest we Forget' being carried by INA volunteers to the Red Fort, Delhi, on the morning of 16 August 1947 102

Plate 29: Crowds at the Red Fort witnessing the flag hoisting by Pandit Jawaharlal Nehru on 16 August 1947 102
Plate 30: Crowd control arrangements between the intersection of Red Fort and Chandni Chowk on 16 August 1947 103
Plate 31: Crowds assembling on 16 August 1947 at the Red Fort 103
Plate 32: Edwina Mountbatten, Nehru and others at the Red Fort 104
Plate 33: Nehru before news photographers at the Red Fort 104

Acknowledgements

Our interest in closely reconstructing the momentous and complex events of 14–17 August 1947 in the Indian subcontinent goes back to our deeper engagement with Partition and its aftermath in South Asia, the subject of a book co-authored by us and published by Routledge in 2000, with a paperback edition in 2002. In revisiting this theme, we have drawn upon its Chapter 2, added new materials, and also made an effort to situate the events in a wider chronological canvas, keeping in view the 75th centenary commemorations of Independence which are underway in India and Pakistan.

We felt the need to do so in view of the significant shifts in popular narratives which have taken place in recent years. Such shifts have tended to divest the historic events of August 1947 of their meaning, attribute new connotations and even misrepresent the role of individual leaders. These shifts in narratives in the domain of 'public history' persuaded us to return to our original interest and present our findings in a reworked, compact and accessible manner for the general reader. We see our effort as providing a work of historical record which gives a close reconstruction of those four momentous days of August 1947 while emphasizing the larger historical context, based upon our extensive archival work in India, Pakistan and the United Kingdom.

In this endeavour we have incurred many debts. We would like to acknowledge Routledge (a part of the Taylor and Francis Group); the wonderful 'team' at Primus Books, consisting of B.N. Varma, Prasun Chatterjee and Jyotika Mansata, for their advice and support at every step; and to Amrita Ajay, Lee Pei Yuan and Rupak Kumar for their exceptional research and editorial support. We are also thankful to the Nehru Memorial Museum & Library and the Photo Division of the Ministry of Information and Broadcasting in New Delhi for their help with copyright permission for some of the photographs reproduced in the book. We are also grateful to the Nazaria-i-Pakistan Trust for Plates 1–10, for which we have written to them for permission, and we are awaiting their response. We are thankful to the Faculty of Arts & Social Sciences, the South Asian Studies Programme and the Institute of South Asian Studies at the National University of Singapore for providing a congenial and supportive environment for research and writing.

We have made repeated attempts to reach out to the owners of the copyright material included in this book. Most have graciously granted permission gratis, and to them we express our sincere gratitude. There are a few copyright owners who have not responded to our several requests. To them also we express our gratitude and we hope that they will also be kind enough to offer their permissions gratis since this book is part of our academic pursuit.

For their understanding, support and love, our gratitude is as always to our respective families in Singapore and India. Finally, the usual disclaim applies that we alone are jointly responsible for any errors and omissions of fact or interpretation.

Tan Tai Yong
Gyanesh Kudaisya

Introduction

As India and Pakistan prepared to celebrate their respective Diamond Jubilees in mid-August 2022, elaborate plans were announced by governments in both the countries to suitably commemorate the occasion. India marked the anniversary with an initiative known as *Azadi Ka Amrit Mahotsav* (AKAM) ('Elixir of Energy of Independence', according to the official website).[1] The Government of India announced in March 2021 that the *Mahotsav* will be 'dedicated to the people of India who have not only been instrumental in bringing India thus far in its evolutionary journey but also hold within them the power and potential to enable Prime Minister Narendra Modi's vision of activating India 2.0, fuelled by the spirit of '*Aatmanirbhar Bharat*' ('self-reliant India').[2] Ambitious plans were announced for the *Mahotsav*, which we shall discuss at length below.

In Pakistan, President Arif Alvi kick-started the Diamond Jubilee celebrations in Islamabad in March 2022 with the launch of a logo. Referring to what he called India's 'current hate campaign . . . against Muslims', the president reminded fellow Pakistanis that 'the two-nation theory of founding father Quaid-e-Azam Muhammad Ali Jinnah has proved to be true'.[3] He continued: 'The commemoration will therefore remind the new generations of Pakistanis about the very contours of this two-nation theory.'[4] In a similar vein, the then prime minister Imran Khan wanted the celebrations to reflect pride in the achievements of the nation and to recall and reaffirm the ideals of *Quaid-e-Azam* Muhammad Ali Jinnah and Allama Iqbal.[5]

In recent years, academic writings have focused attention on the study of historical anniversaries which commemorate independence or national days. 'Independence Day ceremonies deserve serious scholarly attention', urges David Cannadine, a British historian well known for his writings on invented traditions, political ritual, courtly culture and 'Ornamentalism'.[6] In Cannadine's view, the 'ceremonies marking India's independence in 1947 provided a prototype and model', although he adds that the 'consensus displayed at Independence was in many ways superficial and the pomp and partying concealed continuing tensions and paradoxes'.[7] Likewise, the South Asian historian Yasmin Khan observes that 'the ritual and rhetoric of Independence Day celebrations in New Delhi and Karachi masked confusion about the kinds of state coming into existence and complex new questions about nationality and citizenship that would take a long time to resolve'.[8] The historian Jim Masselos has looked at nationalist and state rituals in the context of the evolution of Independence Day and Republic Day celebrations in India.[9] For several other Asian countries emerging from the shadows of colonialism, studies looking at political symbolism and rituals marking independence or national days provide valuable insights.[10]

It is noteworthy that the meanings of celebrations and remembrances relating to Independence and Partition in India and Pakistan have not remained static but have changed over the decades. The anniversaries offer a valuable opportunity for historians, and the public at large, to reassess the ways in which events and individuals have been written about and remembered or, for that matter, excluded or forgotten. Commemorations also reflect changing contexts and concerns and are so often used by the governments of the day to advance their agendas and to drive home key political messages. In the ensuing paragraphs we briefly look at the tone and content of celebrations of Independence and Partition in India and Pakistan at the milestone anniversaries of the 10th, 25th and 50th anniversaries, marked in 1957, 1972 and 1997, respectively, as also the 75th anniversary being celebrated during 2022–3, so that we may consider how the meanings of the commemorations have changed over time.

In August 1957 India marked its 10th anniversary of Independence in a relaxed, peaceful, and celebratory mood. It was evident that the ruling Congress party, led by Jawaharlal Nehru, continued to enjoy legitimacy as the party that had led the struggle for freedom as well as immense electoral popularity, having won 371 out of 494 parliamentary seats in the elections held earlier that year. Despite the calamitous aftermath of Partition and the immense challenges of building a new nation, Nehru's government had strived hard to keep the country united and politically intact. While economic challenges remained paramount, the country was still basking in the afterglow of Independence. In his speech to mark the occasion, Nehru appealed for unity and a peaceful approach to facing national challenges faced by the nascent nation-state. His speech reflected the nation's priorities in the approaching second decade of Independence—political unity, economic development, and uplift of the material conditions of poverty-stricken masses.[11] On the fraught relations with Pakistan, Nehru struck a conciliatory and confident tone, emphasizing the mutual benefits of friendship, while reminding the people that India would not yield to threats, nor concede her rights.[12]

Across the border the mood in Pakistan at the start of its eleventh year as a new nation was more muted, tempered by the climate of instability and political ferment. As an editorial in the *Dawn* commented: 'After 10 years, Pakistan is still incomplete . . . . Achievements there have been, and progress is undeniable, but on a material plane. And even there benefit has been confined to a few while the lot of many worsens.'[13]

Fifteen years down the road, in 1972, Independence Day celebrations in India provided yet another opportunity to reflect on the nation's journey since 1947. In her message, Prime Minister Indira Gandhi described it as 'a quarter century packed with trial and challenge, by overcoming which the nation has emerged stronger, is more cohesive and more determined to reach its goal—justice and equality of opportunity for all'.[14] The highlight of the 1972 celebrations was the special midnight session of the Indian parliament at which the 'mood was of great rejoicing, together with remembrances of leaders and comrades who are no more'. The 'nation rededicated itself to its cherished goals of unity, democracy, socialism and secularism'.[15]

The session saw the presence of twenty veterans from the Constituent Assembly who joined in the visitors' gallery. A portrait of Dr B.R. Ambedkar, widely acknowledged as the moving spirit behind the drafting of the Indian Constitution, was unveiled in the Central Hall. In her address from Delhi's seventeenth-century Red Fort, Indira Gandhi paid 'tributes to the unity shown by the people which led to the victory against Pakistan in the recent military conflict'.[16] She declared that it was 'not merely a military victory but a victory of the noble ideals that India cherished all these years'.[17] She recalled the valour of those who sacrificed their lives in the war for the liberation of Bangladesh.

Similar sentiments were echoed in the events in different state capitals and union territories. In Bombay, at a function held at the Azad Maidan, over 2,000 freedom fighters were honoured. At Poona the highlight of the celebrations was a torchlight procession through the streets of the city. The central government announced plans to grant amnesty and order the release 4,000 prisoners serving long sentences. Plans were also announced to establish 5,000 'Jayanti Villages' in community blocks across the country, to serve as a lasting monument to the Silver Jubilee. It was envisaged that a hundred houses would be built for Harijans in each 'Jayanti Village' with a primary school, drinking water, electricity and other amenities. In yet another ambitious plan, the central government announced that it would set up 'Bharat Bhavans' in each state capital and union territory to project the nation's 'unity in diversity'. Libraries and resource centres would be set up with books, records, pictures and films about different regions of India.

The Silver Jubilee functions did not pass without voices of dissent being raised. Critics contrasted the then ongoing celebrations to the hardships faced by the poor due to persistent conditions of severe drought across several states. In the Bihar legislature, the special session was marked by pandemonium as Socialist legislators shouted '*Yeh azadi jhooti hai, desh ki janata bhooki hai!*' (This independence is a farce; the people of the country are still hungry!).[18] In Trivandrum, Kerala, the Communist leader E.M.S. Namboodiripad declared that his party would boycott the celebrations as these 'sought to give official recognition to the betrayal perpetuated by selfish men who rose to power in the name of the untold sacrifices by thousands of martyrs and freedom fighters'.[19] In New Delhi, the Socialist parliamentarian, Samar Guha, boycotted the midnight parliamentary session to protest against the neglect shown to the sacrifices of Subhash Chandra Bose by not placing his portrait in the Parliament's Central Hall.

On 15 August 1973, the year-long Silver Jubilee celebrations concluded, although on a note of controversy. Before her customary speech from the

Red Fort's ramparts, Indira Gandhi consigned to a 32-ft underground pit a stainless-steel vault containing a 'time-capsule' which contained for posterity a record of achievements of twenty-five years of independent India.[20] Inscribed on copper plates, its text had been prepared by a historian selected by the government's Indian Council of Historical Research. Several parliamentarians and historians raised questions over the 'veracity of the contents' which was alleged to be 'distorted and partial'.[21] Following the end of the 'Emergency', after Mrs Gandhi lost power, the Janata government ordered that the 'time-capsule' be exhumed, and its contents subjected to scrutiny. Although the vault was retrieved in December 1977, its contents have never been made public.[22]

Not unexpectedly, the commemoration of the landmark Golden Jubilee in 1997 was marked with exuberance, enthusiasm and fervour, with the spotlight turned on the story of South Asia's destiny since 1947. The themes then highlighted were: How has the region fared since the end of colonial rule? What have its people done with the freedom they achieved after bitter turmoil and sacrifice? As a part of the celebrations in New Delhi, over 25,000 people in costumes of twenty-five different states and in colours of the national flag, marched from India Gate on the 3 km. route to reach President's House where Prime Minister Inder Kumar Gujral received them. Another highlight was a special midnight session of Parliament, with the singing of the national anthem and a two-minute silence to honour the memory of the martyrs of the freedom struggle. A short excerpt from a speech by Mahatma Gandhi was relayed, followed by Jawaharlal Nehru's 'Tryst with Destiny' speech, which was recreated almost to the minute fifty years after it had been delivered. An address by the then newly elected President K.R. Narayanan followed, urging people to build social movements to fight 'poverty, population growth and environmental degradation'.[23] The following morning, on 15 August 1997, Prime Minister Gujral raised the tricolour over Delhi's Red Fort, in a tradition dating back to the first Independence Day. A fly-past of fighter jets produced smoke plumes of white, saffron and green, the colours of the national flag, as Gujral rose to make his speech in which he paid rich tributes to those who had struggled against colonial rule.

Across the border in Pakistan the celebrations were heralded by a special midnight session of the National Assembly in which the then Prime Minister Nawaz Sharif envisioned a 'glorious future' for the country. He recalled how Pakistan had to face aggression when it had just begun its journey and declared that the nation, having survived the trauma of its birth and the obstacles, thereafter, had now become invincible.[24] The following morning, at a special ceremony outside Parliament in Islamabad, the national flag was hoisted with a thirty-one gun salute. In the provincial capitals of Karachi, Lahore, Quetta and Peshawar similar ceremonies took place with twenty-one gun salvos. Sirens alerted the people in all major cities to the ceremonies, which included a minute's nation-wide silence in the memory of those who had sacrificed their lives for the creation and preservation of Pakistan. The focal point of the events was the Mausoleum of the *Quaid-i-Azam* Mohammad Ali Jinnah in Karachi, where an impressive and colourful change of guard ceremony took place. Wreaths were laid and *fateha* prayers offered by dignitaries and common people alike as they visited the *mazar*. In Lahore, Nawaz Sharif and other leaders visited the tomb of poet-philosopher Allama Mohammad Iqbal, widely regarded as the spiritual inspiration behind the idea of a separate homeland for Muslims in the subcontinent. In separate messages the president and prime minister urged the people to 'help eliminate prejudice, ignorance and corruption' and contribute to the effort 'to build a modern progressive state with a sound scientific and economic basis and social justice'.[25]

While these official functions were the highlights, the celebrations were by no means confined to these events as popular expressions of national pride took diverse forms in both India and Pakistan. In the federal capitals of Islamabad and Delhi, buildings were illuminated with neon lights and archways were put up at prominent crossings and markets with salutations and portraits of national leaders. Shops, markets, and houses were bedecked with flags, colourful buntings and national emblems. From dawn, volunteer groups went around city neighborhoods collecting people for flag-hoisting ceremonies. Children's choirs sang the national anthem and patriotic songs and bands performed in parks. Concerts, poetry sessions, folk dances and musical extravaganzas were organized in many cities. Floats depicting regional cultural motifs featured prominently in rallies which took place everywhere. Throughout Pakistan special prayers were offered in mosques during congregational worship for the nation's progress, solidarity and integrity. Multitudes flocked to the memorials of Jinnah and Gandhi in Karachi and Delhi to pay their homage to the *Quaid-i-Azam* and the 'Father of the Nation', respectively. At many functions, pigeons were released to signify freedom from bondage. In Delhi's Walled City, the residents followed the tradition of kite-flying and at night tens of thousands of children lit candles and oil lamps, and the sky was rent with deafening blasts of crackers and a massive display of fireworks. Torchlight processions took place in many areas and, in at least two cities, residents formed human chains as a symbol of unity.

Amidst the soul-stirring scenes in both India and Pakistan, the occasion of the fiftieth anniversary of independence brought about a sense of deep introspection and stock-taking. There was, first, an effort to work out a 'balance sheet' of national achievements and failures since 1947. The half-centennial became the occasion to introspect and come to terms with the phenomenon of Partition—'the other face of freedom'—as the people of India and Pakistan have come to look upon it.

As India approached the 75th anniversary of Independence and Partition ambitious plans were, once again, drawn to commemorate the milestone. Indian Prime Minister Narendra Modi kick-started the 75th anniversary celebrations at the historic Sabarmati Ashram in Ahmedabad on 12 March 2021, declaring the *mahotsav* would be 'dedicated to the people of India who have not only been instrumental in bringing India thus far in its evolutionary journey but also have the power and potential to enable Prime Minister Narendra Modi's vision of activating India 2.0, fueled by the spirit of Aatmanirbhar Bharat ("Self-Reliant India").'[26] The official celebrations of Azadi Ka Amrit Mahotsav, the highpoint of which was 15 August 2022, would continue till 15 August 2023.

In the prime minister's speeches and writings, the term *Amrit Kaal* has figured frequently. By this he designates a specific period of India between the years 2022 to 2047 which would mark the centenary of Indian Independence. The term comes from Vedic astrology, in which *Amrit Kaal* is a critical epoch in India's millenia-old history where 'the gate of greater pleasure is opened for the inhuman [(*sic*), non human?], angels and human beings. It is considered to be the best and most auspicious time to start any new task'.[27] This is a reference to deriving the best in every field, making it imperative for everyone to make *prayas* (to strive) for this. Modi stated that the purpose of *Amrit Kaal* is to better the lives of citizens, lessen the developmental divide between villages and cities and reduce government interference in public life. It also entails the development or acquisition of the latest technologies for the country.[28]

Further, Modi declared: 'While India has made rapid strides, there should be a "saturation" of development and 100 per cent accomplishments with every village having roads, every family having a bank account, every eligible person having health insurance and gas connection.'[29] Explaining the significance of the *mahotsav*, Modi stated:

> The Azadi Amrit Mahotsav means elixir of energy of independence; elixir of inspirations of the warriors of freedom struggle; elixir of new ideas and pledges; and elixir of Aatmanirbharta (self reliance). Therefore, this Mahotsav is a festival of awakening of the nation; festival of fulfilling the dream of good governance; and the festival of global peace and development.
>
> . . .
>
> Like the history of the freedom movement, the journey of 75 years after independence is a reflection of the hard work, innovation, enterprise of ordinary Indians. Whether in the country or abroad, we Indians have proved ourselves with our hard work. We are proud of our Constitution. We are proud of our democratic traditions. The mother of democracy, India is still moving forward by strengthening democracy. India, rich in knowledge and science, is leaving its mark from Mars to the moon.[30]

Under the rubric of AKAM, five broad themes have been delineated around which the celebrations are being organized.[31] Under the first theme 'Freedom Struggle', commemorations, events and remembrances of 'unsung heroes' are the focus. For example, 'Birsa Munda Jayanti Divas', 'Declaration of Provisional Government of Free India' by Subhas Chandra Bose, etc. The second theme relates to 'Ideas@75' and the events envisaged include Kashi Utsav (a literary festival at Varanasi) and 'Postcards to Prime Minister', under which 75 lakh children were encouraged to write their ideas and vision of India in 2047. The third theme relates to 'Resolve@75' under which 'collective resolve, well laid-out action plans, and determined efforts to translate ideas into actions' are the focus. The fourth theme, 'Action@75', relates to 'efforts to help India take its rightful position in the new world order emerging in a post Covid world' and steps taken to implement policies.[32] Finally, under 'Achievements@75', efforts are underway to showcase the 'evolution and progress across different sectors' and to provide 'a public account of our collective achievements as a 75-year-old independent country with a legacy of 5000+ years of ancient history'.[33]

Different departments and agencies of the central and state governments in India have announced a spate of initiatives to mark the start of 'Amrit Kaal'. For example, Modi launched for the first time in India's currency history, a special series of coins that are 'visually-impaired friendly'.[34] These are not just commemorative but are for everyday circulation. While launching them, Modi expressed the hope that they would 'remind people of the goal of Amrit Kaal and motivate' them.[35] The central government also announced a special remission scheme for prisoners. Under this, the first lot of eligible prisoners were released in a phased manner on 15 August 2022, with subsequent batches of releases scheduled for 26 January 2023 and finally 15 August 2023.[36] On 21 June 2022, Modi inaugurated the Chess Olympiad Torch Relay covering seventy-five cities in India and ending in Chennai, where between 28 July and 10 August 2022 the Chess Olympiad was hosted by the Government of Tamil Nadu.[37]

In another significant initiative on 5 August 2022, Home Minister Amit Shah launched a 'mega historical' tele-serial *titled Swaraj: Bharat Ke Swatantrata Sangram Ki Samagra Gatha* (Swaraj: The Complete Tale of India's Freedom Struggle). Consisting of hour-long episodes to be broadcast over seventy-five weeks, the serial aims to highlight 'the glorious history of India's freedom struggle and lesser-known tales about Indian history'. The state broadcaster Doordarshan is carrying out its broadcast every Sunday in English, Hindi and nine other regional languages.[38]

While the spirit of exuberance and buoyancy which characterizes these ongoing celebrations is noteworthy, one cannot fail to acknowledge, even within the time span of the seventy-five weeks of the *mahotsav*, the many deeper and widespread challenges which face people and society in India. Perhaps the starkest challenge manifested itself in the public health crisis triggered by the outbreak of the Delta variant of the Covid-19 pandemic. Between April and June 2021, as the variant spread across cities, towns and villages, media reports drew attention to the virtual collapse of the healthcare infrastructure across the country. It was widely reported that hospitals were unable to provide emergency oxygen for respiratory support to critically ill patients. There was an alarming shortage of hospital beds and widespread concerns were also raised at the shortage of vaccines, their delay and uneven rollouts across different states. All these called into question the government's claims of having an effective, welfare-oriented anti-Covid strategy in place. Further, enormous economic hardships faced by the common people, especially migrant workers in cities, resulting from the economic shutdown and loss of jobs in the wake of Covid-19, have been widely reported in the media.

Further, the spirit of the *mahotsav* also came to be dampened by the intense, widespread and prolonged farmers' protest, the longest in modern Indian history, which engulfed the north Indian states of Punjab, Haryana, western Uttar Pradesh and parts of Rajasthan, and also saw protest marches further afield in states like Maharashtra, Tamil Nadu and Kerala. The protests were organized by farmers' unions against the hasty and arbitrary enactment of three farm laws passed by Parliament in September 2020.[39] This measure triggered strong protests, initially in Punjab and Haryana, which soon spread to other states. The farmers' unions showed remarkable solidarity through their sustained movement which highlighted long-standing challenges facing the crisis-ridden agricultural sector. The unions drew attention to the rising input costs, declining productivity, unwillingness of the government to provide the minimum support price for farm produce and the mounting debt burden—issues which had led to a large number of farmer suicides in the past in states like Maharashtra, Karnataka and elsewhere. Taking note of the farmers' protest, the Supreme Court stayed the implementation of the farm laws in January 2021. Not satisfied by this, the protesters gave a call for '*Dilli Chalo!*' (March to Delhi!). Organized as 'Farmer's Parade' on the occasion of the Republic Day on 26 January 2021, it saw tens of thousands of farmers march with their tractors and converge at various entry points en route the national capital. Some of the convoys deviated from pre-sanctioned police routes and reached the Red Fort to install their flag on the mast of its ramparts. Sit-in protests continued for several months, including through the severe winter, at Singhu, Tikri, Ghazipur and Shahjahanpur, the four entry points into the national capital. Through much of the *Amrit Mahotsav*, these protests continued. Only after the farm laws were unilaterally repealed by the union government, did the farmers withdraw their protest, after a campaign which they sustained for over one year and four months, in which a large number of protesters lost their lives, with death estimates varying between 537 and 750. Although the farmers peacefully withdrew their movement, the deeper challenges arising from the impact of climate change on agriculture, the growing disparity of incomes between the city and the countryside, the reluctance of the state to provide subsidies to the farm sector and the sustainability of agriculture as the mainstay of the Indian economy, continue to confront India, with no easy solutions in sight. Ironically, none of these concerns have even been taken up in the discourse surrounding *Amrit Mahotsav.*

In the run-up to 15 August 2022, a *Har Ghar Tiranga* ('Tricolour Atop Every Home') campaign was launched by Modi. Coinciding with the climax of the *Amrit Mahotsav*, it aimed to get 20 crore households across the country to hoist the Tricolour for three days between 13 and 15 August 2022. The stated aim of the *Tiranga* campaign was:

to encourage people to bring the Tiranga home and to hoist it to mark the 75th year of India's independence. Our relationship with the flag has always been more formal and institutional than personal. Bringing the flag home collectively as a nation in the 75th year of independence thus becomes symbolic of not only an act of personal connection to the Tiranga but also an embodiment of our commitment to nation-building. The idea behind the initiative is to invoke the feeling of patriotism in the hearts of the people and to promote awareness about the Indian National Flag.[40]

The government has amended the 'Flag Code of India', making it possible for the flag to be made using polyester, cotton, wool, silk and *khadi* bunting materials.[41] It also removed size restrictions on the flag. Official sources indicated that the flag would be made available at 1.6 lakh post offices across the country as well as e-commerce platforms. Critics have expressed concerns over the use of polyester and machine-made cloth as symbolizing a break with *khadi*, its intimate connections with the life and work of the Father of the Nation and with the legacy of the freedom movement.[42] Scholars draw attention to the rich symbolism of *khadi*. The anthropologist Emma Tarlo writes: 'To Gandhi, khadi was more than simply cloth; it was the material embodiment of an ideal, representing freedom from the yoke of colonialism, and standing for economic self-sufficiency, political independence, spiritual humility, moral purity, national integrity, communal unity, social equality, a challenge to untouchability, and the embrace of non-violence.'[43]

Critics point out that the change in the Flag Code also signifies other key changes. According to Lt. Gen. Prakash Menon, a retired defense strategist, the change in the Flag Code also marks a 'conceptual shift from the collective to the individual platform'.[44] It has been pointed out that only the upper-class households would have the means to purchase, maintain and hoist the national flag. Concerns have also been raised on its effect on climate change and on its proper disposal.[45]

Having considered, at some length, how India and Pakistan have commemorated Independence and Partition at the critical milestones of its tenth, twenty-fifth and fiftieth, and seventy-fifth anniversaries, we can now turn our attention in the pages that follow to the events of 14–17 August 1947 as they then unfolded.

Notes

1. Official website, see https://amritmahotsav.nic.in/index.htm, accessed 4 August 2022. The term literally means 'elixir of life'.
2. Ibid.
3. The *Nation*, 8 March 2022. Also, Ministry of Information and Broadcasting, Government of Pakistan, 'Press Release', 7 March 2022, see http://www.moib.gov.pk/News/44832, accessed 2 August 2022.
4. Ibid.
5. Ibid.
6. David Cannadine, 'Introduction: Independence Day Ceremonials in Historical Perspective', *The Round Table*, vol. 97, no. 398, 2008, pp. 649–65. Also published as Introduction to *The Iconography of Independence: 'Freedoms at Midnight'*, ed. Robert Holland, Susan Williams and Terry Barringer, London and New York: Routledge, 2010, pp. 1–17.

7. Ibid.
8. Yasmin Khan, 'The Ending of an Empire: From Imagined Communities to Nation States in India and Pakistan', *The Round Table*, vol. 97, no. 398, 2008, pp. 695–704. Also see Chandrika Kaul, 'At the Stroke of the Midnight Hour: Lord Mountbatten and the British Media at Indian independence', *The Round Table*, vol. 97, no. 398, 2008, pp. 677–93.
9. Jim Masselos, 'The Magic Touch of Being Free', in *India: Creating a Modern Nation*, ed. Jim Masselos, New Delhi: Sterling Publishers, 1988. Also see his 'India's Republic Day: The Other 26 January', *South Asia*, vol. 19, Special Issue, 1996, pp. 1–14.
10. See, for example, Lily Kong and Brenda S.A. Yeoh, 'The Construction of National Identity through the Production of Ritual and Spectacle: An Analysis of National Day Parades in Singapore', *Political Geography*, vol. 16, no. 3, 1997, pp. 213–39; A.J. Stockwell, 'Merdeka! Looking Back at Independence Day in Malaysia, 31 August 1957', in *The Iconography of Independence: 'Freedoms at Midnight'*, ed. Robert Holland, Susan Williams and Terry Barringer, London and New York: Routledge, 2010, pp. 113–30; and Brij V. Lal, 'Of Ruptures and Recuperations: Fiji's Fifty Years of Independence', *Journal of Pacific History*, vol. 36, no. 2, 2021, pp. 185–97. Also see Carola Lentz and David Lowe, *Remembering Independence*, London and New York: Routledge, 2018.
11. *New York Times*, 15 August 1957.
12. *Times of India*, 16 August 1957.
13. Ibid., 15 August 1957.
14. Ibid., 14, 15 and 16 August 1972.
15. Ibid.

16. Ibid.
17. Ibid.
18. Ibid.
19. Ibid., 15 and 16 August 1972.
20. Ibid., 16 August 1973.
21. K.S. Dakshina Murthy, 'After Indira Gandhi in 1973, India's Tryst with Second Time Capsule', *The Federal*, 28 July 2020, see https://thefederal.com/features/after-indira-gandhi-in-1973-indias-tryst-with-second-time-capsule/, accessed 4 August 2022.
22. *Times of India*, 9 December 1977.
23. Cited in Tan Tai Yong and Gyanesh Kudaisya, *The Aftermath of Partition in South Asia*, London: Routledge, 2000, p. 3
24. *Dawn*, 14 and 15 August 1997.
25. Cited in Tan and Kudaisya, *The Aftermath of Partition*, p. 8.
26. ANI, 'Amit Shah Calls upon People to Join "Har Ghar Tiranga" Programme', *The Print*, 2 August 2022, see https://theprint.in/india/amit-shah-calls-upon-people-to-join-har-ghar-tiranga-programme/1066407/, accessed 4 August 2022.
27. Anisha Joneja, 'Union Budget 2022–3: What Does "Amrit Kaal" Mean?', *Deccan Herald*, 1 February 2022, see https://www.deccanherald.com/business/union-budget/union-budget-2022-23-what-does-amrit-kaal-mean-1076822.html, accessed 4 August 2022.
28. Ibid.
29. Ibid.
30. See https://amritmahotsav.nic.in/, accessed 4 August 2022.
31. Ibid. The New Delhi-based Observer Research Foundation has taken up these themes to reflect their

policy implications. See Samir Saran, ed., *India at 75: Aspirations, Ambitions and Approaches*, New Delhi: Observer Research Foundation, 2022.

32. Saran, ed., *India at 75*.
33. Ibid.
34. PTI, 'PM Modi Launches New Series of Coins with Azadi ka Amrit Mahotsav Design', *Business Standard*, 6 June 2022, see https://www.business-standard.com/article/current-affairs/pm-modi-launches-new-series-of-coins-with-azadi-ka-amrit-mahotsav-design-122060600752_1.html, accessed 8 August 2022.
35. Ibid.
36. ANI, '"Azadi ka Amrit Mahotsav" Celebration: Centre to release Special Category Prisoners in Three Phases', *FirstPost,* 16 June 2022, see https://www.firstpost.com/india/azadi-ka-amrit-mahotsav-celebration-centre-to-release-special-category-prisoners-in-three-phases-10800871.html, accessed 4 August 2022.
37. ANI, 'Historic Chess Olympiad Torch Relay Covers over 20 Cities across India', *Asian News International*, 29 June 2022, see https://www.aninews.in/news/sports/others/historic-chess-olympiad-torch-relay-covers-over-20-cities-across-india20220629163219/, accessed 4 August 2022.
38. 'HM Amit Shah Launches Doordarshan Serial—"Swaraj: Bharat ke Swatantrata Sangram ki Samagra Gatha"', *All India Radio News Service Division*, see https://newsonair.gov.in/News?title=Home-Minister-Amit-Shah-launches-serial-Swaraj---Bharat-Ke-Swatantrata-Sangram-ki-Samagra-Gatha%3B-Urges-youth-to-take-pride-in-country%26%2339%3Bs-history&id=445507, accessed 10 August 2022.

This move is reminiscent of Doordarshan's broadcasting of the Hindu epic *Ramayan* in 1987 which provided a backdrop to the largest political campaign for Hindutva organized on the question of the construction of a temple dedicated to Lord Ram at Ayodhya. For details see, Arvind Rajagopal, *Politics after Television: Hindu Nationalism and the Reshaping of the Public in India*, Cambridge: Cambridge University Press, 2001.

39. See Natasha Behl, 'India's Farmers' Protest: An Inclusive Vision of Indian Democracy', *American Political Science Review*, 2022, pp. 1–6. See also, Kamaljit K. Sangha, 'The Biggest Peaceful Protest against Corporations in Human History—Daring Farmers of India', *Journal of Agriculture and Ecology Research* Internationa, vol. 22, no. 6, 2021, p. 1 and Amita Baviskar and Michael Levien, 'Farmers' Protests in India: Introduction to the JPS Forum', *The Journal of Peasant Studies*, vol. 48, no. 7, 2021, pp. 1341–55.

40. See https://amritmahotsav.nic.in/har-ghar-tiranga.htm, accessed 12 August 2022.

41. For a nuanced understanding of the changes at different points in time to the Flag Code of India and their underlying meanings, see Srirupa Roy, 'A Symbol of "freedom": The Indian flag and the Transformations of Nationalism, 1906–2002', *The Journal of Asian Studies*, vol. 65, no. 3, 2006, pp. 495–527. See also Arundhati Virmani, 'National Symbols under Colonial Domination', *Past and Present*, vol. 164, 1999, pp. 169–97; Sadan Jha, 'The Indian National Flag as a Site of Daily Plebiscite', *Economic and Political Weekly*, 2008, pp. 102–11; and Sadan Jha, 'Challenges in the History of Colours: The Case of Saffron', *The Indian*

Economic and Social History Review, vol. 51, no. 2, 2014, pp. 199–229.

42. Prakash Menon, 'Har Ghar Tiranga is a Good Idea, but Not Every Indian Has the Means to Follow the Indian Flag Code', *The Print*, 2 August 2022, see https://theprint.in/opinion/har-ghar-tiranga-is-a-good-idea-but-not-every-indian-has-the-means-to-follow-flag-code/1064181/, accessed 4 August 2022; Jyoti Punwani, 'The Amended Flag Code: A Farewell to Khadi', *Deccan Herald*, 18 July 2022, see https://www.deccanherald.com/opinion/the-amended-flag-code-a-farewell-to-khadi-1127733.html, accessed 12 August 2022.
43. Emma Tarlo, 'Khadi', in *Key Concepts in Modern Indian Studies*, ed. Rachel Dwyer et al., New York: New York University Press, 2016.
44. Menon, 'Har Ghar Tiranga is a Good Idea'.
45. Ibid. 'Due to their price competitiveness and ease of manufacture. But it is worth remembering that the process of making a T-shirt from polyester emits more than twice as much carbon as making it from cotton. If the polyester flag industry becomes popular, India's commitment to reducing carbon emissions in the fight against climate change could suffer a setback.'

14–17 August 1947 and the Celebration of Independence

Clock-hands joined palms in respectful greetings…

When the Bombay-born author Salman Rushdie crafted these words in his celebrated novel *Midnight's Children* to signify the countdown to the midnight ceremonies which heralded the advent of Indian Independence, he was drawing upon an imagery about the meanings and memories of the events of 14–17 August 1947 which is powerfully embedded in the popular imagination in the Indian subcontinent. Indeed, textbook histories in both India and Pakistan give a prominent place to this historic landmark in terms of signifying the end of British colonial rule and the emergence of India and Pakistan in the international arena as sovereign nation-states.[1] Unsurprisingly, South Asian historians have looked upon it as a twentieth-century turning point, the moment of 'fulfilment' of a historic movement 'comparable in its sweep, its complexity and its consequences to the Russian Revolution of 1917, or the emergence of a revitalized China in 1949'.[2] These textbook accounts typically focus on the official ceremonies which marked the transfer of power, the stirring speeches of Jawaharlal Nehru and Muhammad Ali Jinnah to mark the occasion and the unprecedented celebrations which took place across the subcontinent. They also talk about the tragedy of Partition and mention in passing the mass violence and large-scale suffering of the uprooted: such events are largely described in terms of the 'birth pangs' of the 'nation'.

Yet, outside history books, the memories of the coming of Independence remain deeply etched in peoples' minds. It is ironic that these memories are mostly not about the events which are celebrated in textbook histories but about individuals and family circumstances, their hopes and fears, and about the anxieties which many people, especially from the 'minority' communities, felt about the future. Further, while attempting to reconstruct the happenings of 14–17 August 1947, one is struck by not just the enormous diversity of the events but also their epic quality and the sheer futility of narrating them within a single frame as has often been the endeavour of history textbooks which locate these events within the narrowly-framed univocal narrative of the 'nation-state'.

The ceremonies, rituals and events of 14–17 August 1947 were experienced by millions throughout the subcontinent.[3] It is possible to recapture, although only partially, the moods and emotions of people who participated in these events or witnessed them by drawing upon a range of sources such as autobiographical accounts, newspaper reports, memoirs and oral history narratives. There also exist representations of these events in the literature of at least half a dozen Indian languages, besides English, as well as in films and other visual media. Even a mere exploration of these reveal that the meanings and memories of the events are constructed quite differently from the narratives which staple history textbooks seek to convey. It is now well recognized that to an overwhelming number of people across much of the northern and eastern parts of the subcontinent, the event signified Partition (*vibhajan* or *batwara*) rather than the coming of Independence (*azadi*). In the more than fifty years which have since elapsed, this bipolarity in the reconstruction of the event has been accentuated.

The official Independence Day ceremonies which take place every year in India and Pakistan, a day apart, commemorate the moment of the birth of the Nation.[4] With the raising of the flag and the singing of the anthem, the ceremonies in both New Delhi and Islamabad remind the citizens of the sacrifices of the 'freedom fighters' and urge them to realize the lofty vision of the 'founding fathers'. In this sense, the state rituals have served to perpetuate only one aspect of the momentous events of August 1947. In doing so, they have effaced the range of meanings and memories of the events which lurk in popular memory.

Moving away from such representations, this book attempts to reconstruct the momentous events of 14–17 August 1947 by adopting a 'slice of life' approach to how the occasion was experienced by common people.

The discussion begins by looking at how the ceremonies and rituals for Independence were planned. Then, ideas about how to organize the events as well as the manner in which the format of the ceremonies evolved are explored. From here we move on to investigate the notion of 'celebration'. The widely diverging perceptions of the approaching event are described. The narrative which follows focuses on the experiences of those who participated in the consecration rituals performed to mark the birth of the 'nation'. Here, the examples of several important cities are used to convey the moods and sentiments that prevailed then. There appear to be significant differences in the ways in which different cities and towns in the subcontinent marked the event. At these places, diverse communities responded to the event differently. It is argued that perceptions of what this historical landmark signified were determined by the location, both physical and social, of the individuals concerned. Further, the case is made that there was more to the events of 14–17 August 1947 than can be refracted through the bipolar categorical artifices of *azadi* and *batwara*, and an attempt is made to unravel the profusion of complex and ambiguous meanings attached to these terms. In doing so, divergent voices emerge which present contested visions of Independence, nationhood and citizenship.

Preparing for the 'Appointed Day'

We begin this discussion by first looking at how the state ceremonies were planned by top British officials in

New Delhi in close consultation with the 'inheritors', the apex leaders of the Indian National Congress and the Muslim League. The action began in New Delhi in Viceroy Louis Mountbatten's Secretariat. As the pages of his tear-down calendar ran down and the 'appointed day' approached, the attention of Mountbatten's staff turned towards planning the official ceremonies to mark the transfer of power.[5] By early July 1947 their plans had evolved and the details for the key events were being finalized. On 18 July 1947 the Viceroy reported to London that 'progress has been made on the plans for official ceremonies on the transfer of power'. In his final week as the last British Viceroy of India, Mountbatten's calendar included a day trip to Karachi on 14 August for the transfer-of-power ceremonies in Pakistan and similar inaugural ceremonies in Delhi which he was much more enthusiastic about (as he was being sworn in as the first Governor General of independent India). How these ceremonies were to be organized and the form each of these was to take became clear as close consultations took place with Congress and Muslim League leadership. For instance, Mountbatten reported the Pakistani leadership's request that on 14 August, 'as Ramzan will still be on, Jinnah has asked that I should stay to a State Dinner, so that I will defer my departure'.[6] The Viceregal staff had to deal with questions of constitutional propriety as well as sensitive matters of protocol.

In planning the ceremonies, a specific assurance that Mountbatten secured from the incumbent leadership was that 'the Ceremony of substituting the new Dominion flag for the Union Jack will not be performed'. Further, it was specifically arranged that 'the Union Jack over the old Lucknow Residency, which has never been lowered by day or night, will be hauled down quite unostentatiously at sundown on 14 August and sent home'.[7] Then, there were several nitty-gritty details which needed to be sorted out. For instance, there was the issue of the alteration of the King's Title by omission of the term 'Emperor of India' and his signature to be 'GR' and not 'GRI'.[8] As these were dealt with over the weeks, London conveyed its approval of the plans generally, and agreed to send a message on behalf of the king for the occasion.[9] It was agreed that 'similar ceremonies will, however, not take place at Residencies in the Indian States where they exist'. This was not surprising, given the ambiguous position of the princely states and the question of how people in these states might take part in the ceremonies being organized throughout the subcontinent. Ian Copland has shown that there existed great uncertainty within the princely states in terms of their 'integration' with either India or Pakistan. He notes that, 'contrary to popular belief, Mountbatten did not achieve anything approaching the '"full basket" of accessions'. On the eve of Independence, a number of states across the subcontinent, including Hyderabad, Kashmir, Indore, Jodhpur and Rampur, had failed to declare their intentions. The sense of disquiet which people in these parts experienced over their uncertain future could well be imagined. Consequently, the rituals of Independence, as they had been planned in the rest of the subcontinent, could not be observed in these areas.[10]

In working out the details of the New Delhi

ceremonies, the Viceroy held close consultations with Jawaharlal Nehru and his Congress party colleagues. It was arranged that there were to be three ceremonies with rather distinct meanings and symbolism. First was a midnight ceremony at which the Indian Constituent Assembly would meet in a special session to declare that it had assumed responsibility of government in Free India. Then, a ceremony the following morning where 'a Proclamation will be made by the Governor General, who will be accompanied by Lady Mountbatten to the assembled Constituent Assembly of the Union of India . . . and a message from H.M. The King would be read'. Finally, an inter-services parade that evening was planned as an outdoor event to enable the citizens of the capital to participate in the celebrations. These three key ceremonies set the format which was adopted by those in charge of organizing the celebrations in the provincial capitals and other cities. 'It is intended that ceremonies in the Provinces will be on much the same lines as those at Delhi and Karachi.'

In their dealings with Congress leaders for planning the official ceremonies for the Indian dominion, the Viceroy and his staff came up with vexing problems of astrology. Mountbatten complained that:

> The astrologers are being rather tiresome since both the 13th and 15th have been declared inauspicious days, whereas the 14th is auspicious. I was not warned that I ought to consult the astrologers before fixing the day for the transfer of power, but luckily this has been got over by the CA [Constituent Assembly] deciding to meet before midnight on the auspicious fourteenth and take over power as midnight strikes which is apparently still an auspicious moment.

One or two of the more superstitious members of the Cabinet wished to have all the ceremony done at midnight in the Durbar Hall, but as, fortunately, the older members of the cabinet usually go to bed at 9 o'clock, Sleep won the swearing-in battle over Superstition; and we are now going to have the swearing-in ceremony in the presence of 500 people at 8.30 on the morning of the 15th, after which we will all proceed to the CA which I am to address in their new capacity as the LA [Legislative Assembly] of India.[11]

There were other awkward matters too, such as Mahatma Gandhi's decision to stay away from all state ceremonies. Mountbatten complained that the Mahatma's absence was 'intentional', as he 'has never given the June plan his unqualified blessing'. In view of his well-publicized opposition to Partition, his participation in any form of celebrations might be 'difficult'. Further, according to Mountbatten, Gandhi also 'realises that it would not be possible to fit him into the programme in the way to which he would feel himself entitled'.[12]

A major preoccupation of the Viceroy in the planning of these celebrations related to the question of the design of flags of the two new dominions. He required that 'the Dominions flags should have the Union Jack in the upper canton of their flags as do other members of the Commonwealth'. He felt that 'as flags were an important outward and visible symbol', they would serve to signify the continuity of the British connection through the Commonwealth. Mountbatten, who had a deep personal interest in the design of heraldry and insignia, spent considerable energy trying to persuade Nehru and Jinnah to agree to this proposal, and personally prepared the design of the flags which he handed over with much enthusiasm to them.

However, the idea was rejected by both the Muslim League and the Congress leadership. Jinnah conveyed to Mountbatten that he 'had been unable to find a single supporter for the idea' and claimed that 'it would be repugnant to the religious feelings of the Muslims to have a flag with a Christian cross alongside a Muslim crescent'.[13] When Ismay, the Viceroy's chief of staff, followed up the suggestion with Jinnah, the latter 'pointed out that it would be impossible to have the cross and the crescent on the same flag', as 'all the old hatreds and rivalries would be revived'.[14]

Likewise, and quite predictably, the Congress too rejected the proposal. Nehru explained that 'the general feeling among Congress extremists was that the leaders were pandering far too much to the British' and the incorporation of the Union Jack in the national flag would provoke a strong reaction. Mountbatten realized that the situation had 'reached a point at which it was inadvisable to press the design on them'.[15]

Even so, Mountbatten was not prepared to simply give up. He suggested an alternative procedure by starting 'the custom of hoisting the Union Jack alongside the Dominion flag, either on the same pole or on two separate poles on all special occasions such as birthdays of the Royal Family, Dominion Days . . . and on as many occasions as possible'.[16] For this he received only lukewarm support from both Jinnah and Nehru; the latter 'thought that this scheme would be acceptable if it were not publicised'. Both were 'anxious that this should not be publicised but should simply happen as a matter of routine', as 'they [are] worried about their extremists agitating against over-stressing the British connection, although they are quite willing to retain it themselves'.[17]

Although the planning had been initiated by Mountbatten's staff, the question of preparations for the 15 August 1947 ceremonies was raised during the 14–31 July 1947 session of the Indian Constituent Assembly (CA).[18] Given the Congress party's commitment to the ideals of democracy and republicanism, it was natural that Congress leaders wanted the CA to be the focal point of the transfer-of-power ceremonies, rather than the persona of the Viceroy. Nehru had been very concerned that the ceremonies should not be hijacked by Mountbatten to become a grand finale of imperial ritual for which he had great distaste. On past occasions, he had heaped bitter scorn on these rituals, condemning the British for 'their court ceremonies, their durbars and investitures, their parades, their dinners and evening dress, their pompous utterances'. One way to ensure that the key ceremony had a genuine *nationalist* quality to it was to site it away from the Viceroy's House which Nehru had previously depicted as the 'chief temple where the High Priest officiated'. He assailed the capitol complex in New Delhi itself which provided the setting for the ceremonies as the 'visible symbol of British power, with all its pomp and circumstance and vulgar ostentation and wasteful extravagance'.[19] Nehru and other Congress leaders therefore insisted that the key ceremony should take place not at the Viceroy's House but at the Council House, later to be known as the Parliament House of independent India.

This was, in the view of the Congress leaders, appropriate. In the original plans for New Delhi as the imperial capital, the British had not provided for a separate Council House. They had decided that the Imperial Legislative Council did not need a separate building and could meet under the Viceregal roof. Later, it was thought that the space could be found for it in the Secretariat buildings. However, in subsequent years they had to reluctantly change their plans to erect a separate building in keeping with the 'march of constitutional progress'. The Council House was thus built as an 'afterthought' and its designer Herbert Baker had to wage a real struggle to give some stature and prominence to the building, which was situated at a much lower elevation than the Viceroy's House and the two Secretariat blocks. Further, it was placed at the edge of the grand urban layout of the city.[20] Thus, in the words of Robert Grant Irving, the architectural historian of New Delhi, 'this monument embodied as none other could the fact of India's progress towards constitutional maturity', it was appropriate that 'from a gallery in the great central hall of that very building, a bugler clad in simple cotton khadi would sound a sonorous note on a seashell, a haunting knell for empire and a summons to self-government'.[21]

Once the site was decided, it was agreed that a special midnight session of the Assembly should be held. However, there were some dissenting voices. Mahavir Tyagi, a Congress legislator from the erstwhile

United Provinces (UP), for instance, suggested that the ceremonies of transfer of power should appropriately take place at the Red Fort. Other than the symbolic considerations, a practical reason he offered was that there might be difficulties in accommodating all the people in the assembly chamber. Nonetheless, the overwhelming opinion supported the Council House as the most preferred venue.

Away from official circles, political parties like the Congress and the Muslim League were bracing themselves to mobilize the ground to ensure a befitting popular reception to the coming of freedom. The Congress leadership, for instance, gave much thought to how the ceremonies were to be organized. On 21 July 1947 the Congress Working Committee met at Harijan Colony in New Delhi to work out its plans. The Committee called upon 'the people to celebrate 15 Aug in a fitting and solemn manner'. It characterized the 'ending of British rule in India as an event of historic and world significance which opens the doors of freedom and opportunity to our people and which will have far-reaching consequences in national and international affairs'. At last, the Committee proclaimed that 'the dawn of freedom' was at hand 'for which people have suffered and laboured for generations'. There was also an expression of regret:

> that freedom has come in a manner which does not bring full joy to it, for it is accompanied by the non-accession of some parts of the country and the breaking up of the living unity of India which nature, history and tradition had fashioned and which was firmly tied up with the idea of freedom.

The Committee believe that the destiny of India will yet be realized and that when passions have cooled, a new and stronger unity based on goodwill and cooperation will emerge.[22]

On the practical arrangements for the celebrations, the Working Committee laid down a 'minimum programme' which included several key events: flag hoisting on public and private buildings in the morning, organization of mass meetings in the afternoon to explain the 'significance of the occasion' and a pledge by people to 'dedicate themselves anew to the national cause, and more particularly to the freedom and progress of the backward classes and the common man'.[23] If circumstances permitted, processions and marches could be organized which could converge at mass meetings. The Working Committee called upon 'the people to begin this new era in India's history with courage, discipline and confidence', in order to 'extend full freedom and opportunity to every citizen to whatever religion or class he or she may belong'.[24]

These guidelines for the 'minimum programme' were followed by instructions sent out in a circular to all the Provincial Congress Committees by General Secretary Shankarrao Deo. Congressmen were urged to observe the day when 'India would be fully free to shape her destiny according to the wishes and genius of her people' with 'solemnity, even though our joy at the dawn of freedom would be mixed with pain at the separation of some of our brethren from us. The separation we hope and believe is temporary and short-lived.'[25] Provincial and subordinate Congress committees were directed to arrange flag-hoisting ceremonies at which 'people of all communities may gather and salute the flag of the free and independent India'. Congress committees were free to add to the minimum programme 'according to local conditions and desire'. However, it was specified that 'in provinces or parts of provinces where for the maintenance of communal peace or some similar reason there are bans on public meetings, etc., the celebration programme may be adjusted accordingly'. Further, Congressmen were urged to work closely with government authorities in organizing 'joint celebrations' which will be 'a fitting symbol of the growing oneness of the people and the Government'.[26]

In these weeks, the Congress leadership was inundated with suggestions about how to commemorate the occasion. For instance, it was suggested to J.B. Kripalani, the Congress president, that a 'New Era be introduced on the 15 August 1947.' This suggestion emanated from Lalta Prasad Saksena of Agra College who proposed that 'the existing eras . . . Vikram, Hijri, Christian could be blended into the National Era'. This would 'perpetually commemorate the Independence of our Motherland and immortalise a few of the Nation Builders'. He suggested that the twelve months of the new calendar could be named after nationalist leaders and designated 'Noroaji, Lajpat, Ali, Tilak, Gokhale, Moti or Motilal, Ajmal or Ansari, Das or Chitranjan, Malavi or Malaviya, Tagore, Andrews, Bhagat'. According to the author of the scheme, here was 'a novel and noble idea to nationalise the very thing of our daily life . . . month to month and year after year [*sic*]'.[27]

Another interesting suggestion came from Chajju

Singh, secretary of the Muzaffarnagar District Congress Committee in UP, who wanted a rather dramatic extravaganza of ceremonies in order to 'revitalise' the Congress, 'uplift the morale' of its cadres, and 'kill the opposition of Hindu Mahasabha and the Muslim League'. Singh wrote to Govind Ballabh Pant, the UP premier, that 'I see depression and despondency all round which is very injurious for the future of the Congress organisation.' He attributed this mood of dejection to the acceptance of Partition by the Congress, as a result of which the party was having to face strong opposition from the extreme Hindu Mahasabha as well as the Muslim League.[28]

Once the details of the programme became known, provincial and local Congressmen were galvanized into action. For instance, the UP Congress sent out an important circular with detailed instructions to all its subordinate bodies which laid down the 'dos' and 'do nots' for Congress cadres.[29] It also elaborated the form which the key ceremonies were to take. On the appointed day the ceremonies would begin at 7.30 a.m. when, at a designated place fixed by district or local authorities, the 'national flag' would be hoisted by a minister, parliamentary secretary, legislator, or a district official, and this was to be followed by a police parade to salute the flag. Then, at 10.30 a.m., flag-hoisting functions were to take place at prominent public or private buildings. At such gatherings Congress volunteers were urged to mobilize as many people as possible. People were to be asked to stop work and perform *jhandaabhivadan* (saluting the flag). The message was also to be explicitly conveyed that 'the flag under which they struggled and suffered has emerged *victorious* and has *become the flag of the State* and now onwards will be hoisted over courts, district offices, police stations and tehsils'. Then, at 4.30 p.m. route marches or processions were to be organized, for which all Congress cadres were urged to mobilize large crowds. People were to be encouraged to don the Gandhi cap and, as far as possible, wear khadi. The marches were to conclude in a public meeting at 6 p.m. which was to be attended by government servants. At night public buildings were to be illuminated and people encouraged to decorate their dwellings.

Local organizations were given the flexibility, within the format of this 'minimum programme', to 'extend it and go beyond it'. However, it was made very clear that no clash was to be allowed between 'official' and 'party' functions. Local cadres were instructed to work closely with the district and local authorities to ensure that events went off in an 'orderly and punctual' manner. The cadres were warned that 'at this time attempts are being made to vitiate the atmosphere': 'It is a matter of pity that when real responsibility is coming into our hands, some short-sighted people are misleading the public and creating obstacles *precisely* at the moment when *the permanent foundations of the nation and nationhood* are being laid'.[30] It was regretted that people were being 'excited by communal propaganda and sentiments' when enormous challenges faced all Indians. In the light of this, it was particularly important to celebrate the birth of the 'nation' in a befitting manner:

We have to celebrate 15 August in such a way that people's

psychology is *metamorphosed* into that *befitting the citizens of an independent nation.* We have to explain to them that with the departure of the British our destiny now lies in our own hands. We now have to build a strong and prosperous nation. We have to establish a democratic polity. We have to bestow the means for an abundant livelihood on peasants and working peoples. We have to remove the gross inequities which can be seen in our society and eliminate poverty and unemployment. We have to empower the people. We have to work according to a plan to augment income, provide work, impart universal education and to bring development to the villages. All these aspirations and expectations cannot be fulfilled overnight.[31]

To be able to meet these challenges, people needed to conduct themselves with dignity and honour. In particular, they were warned that 'anyone unwilling to join in this occasion or programme must not be coerced or commented upon' as 'with the coming of freedom our responsibility goes up and we should remember this even more'.

In sharp contrast to the sense of organization and discipline with which the rank and file of the Congress approached the event, the preparations being made by the Muslim League were *ad hoc* and less organized. This was to be expected as Congress cadres were gearing themselves towards inheriting the mantle of an established imperial order, whereas the Muslim League leadership was confronted with the challenge of enacting rituals of consecration in territories which were in the process of seceding from India. Their preoccupation in the weeks preceding the event had been with securing the sinews of the state itself. The sheer problems of logistics involved in establishing the headquarters in Karachi were overwhelming. In the light of such uncertainties the Muslim League leadership could only issue broad guidelines for the celebrations. On 2 August 1947 Liaquat Ali Khan, in his capacity as the General Secretary of the Muslim League, declared: 'It is up to every citizen and organization to devise their own ways of celebrating according to their means, circumstances and available facilities.' He urged the population to fly the Pakistan 'national flag' on all government buildings, private dwellings and places of business. He proposed meetings and processions but appealed, in the same spirit shown by the Congress leaders, that legal restrictions be followed and ban orders not violated.[32]

However, a flag for the new dominion had not yet been adopted! Less than ten days prior to the inauguration of Pakistan, Muslim League cadres did not know which flag they were expected to hoist. In the last week of July 1947, the Sind Minorities Association had proposed a design of a flag for adoption by the Pakistan Constituent Assembly. It consisted of three diagonal stripes: the central one, which was the biggest, was green with a superscription of a crescent and a star, indicating the central place of Muslims in the new nation. On top was placed a red band with the superscription of *Om* representing the Hindu 'minority'. The third white strip at the bottom stood for 'other minorities'. The entire flag was embossed with a full-sized balance 'signifying justice and fairness to all the people of Pakistan'.[33]

However, on 6 August the special correspondent of *Dawn*, based in Delhi, authoritatively claimed to have learned that 'the design of the flag of Pakistan has been finally chosen'. It was to be a 'dark green rectangular flag in the proportion length to breadth of 3:2 with a white vertical bar at the mast, the green portion bearing a white crescent in the centre and a five pointed white heraldic star'. Further, it was specified that the 'size of the white portion being one fourth the size of the flag, nearest the mast, the remainder three fourths being dark green'.[34] The green and the crescent were traditional symbols of Islam, while the vertical white band on the hoist side symbolized the role of religious 'minorities'. According to Akbar Ahmed, the flag's design is a 'symbol of softness, mystery, magic, romance, compassion, hope and promise'. It was only a week later, when the Pakistan Constituent Assembly met in Karachi, that the flag was officially adopted, literally hours before the actual ceremonies!

Likewise, the new state did not have a national anthem at the time of its inauguration. Pakistan had to wait for seven years before a suitable anthem was adopted in August 1954. That year, after an open competition, the poem 'Pak sarzameen shad bad' by Hafeez Jalandhari was chosen as the national anthem. In the light of such uncertainties it was remarkable that the leaders of Pakistan were at all able to gear themselves for the ceremonials.

'A Day of Mourning!'

While these feverish preparations were being made for the transfer-of-power ceremonies, there was gathering in momentum a strong public sentiment which questioned the idea of celebration. Those who subscribed to this mood included diverse groups of people, for instance, the 'Nationalist Muslims', a group of Muslims who were wedded to the 'secular' ideals of the Congress and who had trenchantly opposed the Partition demand of the Muslim League. Then, there were the extreme Hindu nationalists who took the view that the coming event signified vivisection of 'Mother India' and was, thus, an occasion for mourning rather than joy. Finally, and perhaps most importantly, there were ordinary people in Punjab and Bengal—Hindus, Muslims, Sikhs, Christians, Buddhists—who were extremely concerned about what their place would be as 'minorities' in the new nation-states. They were worried about the safety of their lives and property, their right of residence in the new dominions and their status as citizens. Let us consider how some of these groups looked upon the celebrations which were being planned so enthusiastically in Delhi and Karachi.

We begin with the most organized of the groups who interrogated the concept of commemoration. A major campaign against the celebration plans was organized by extreme Hindu nationalist bodies such as the All India Hindu Mahasabha and the Rashtriya Swayamsevak Sangh (RSS). Their chief ideologue was Vinayak Damodar Savarkar, a romantic nationalist figure with radical, right-wing links who had spent long years in British jails. In 1923 he had authored the work *Hindutva: Who is a Hindu?*[35] In this text Savarkar propounded an alternative vision of nationhood which he called 'Hindutva'.[36] Of the three pillars upon which his notion of Hindutva rested—geographical unity, racial features and a common culture—'the notion of territory was at the heart of Savarkar's ideological construct'.[37] In his view, 'a Hindu was therefore an inhabitant of the zone between the rivers, the seas and the Himalayas, so strongly entrenched that no other country in the world is so perfectly designed by the fingers of nature as a geographical unit'.[38]

On the eve of Independence the Hindu nationalists, a substantial political force, were represented not only by organizations such as the Hindu Mahasabha and the RSS, but by its moderate adherents who were a part of the mainstream Indian National Congress.[39] Within Congress circles, the Hindu right wing enjoyed sympathy, not only at the level of individual leaders such as K.M. Munshi, Purushottam Das Tandon and others, but at the grassroots. In Bengal in particular, the provincial Congress had thrown its lot behind Hindu nationalists and there exists strong evidence of close intermingling at the levels of ideas and organization between the two.[40] Further, the organizational strength of the Hindu extremists on the eve of Independence was growing.[41]

Given this strength, the call by the Hindu nationalists to boycott the coming celebrations was a serious challenge to the Congress. Savarkar, the supreme leader of the Hindu right wing, openly declared that celebrations in any form were not called for, as 15 August symbolized not Independence, but the vivisection of the country. The territorial integrity of *Akhand Bharat* ('indivisible India') which had been 'undivided from times immemorial' was now being destroyed. He urged his supporters never to accept Partition, or to recognize Pakistan.[42] Savarkar's call for boycott echoed among supporters of the Hindu right, growing in numbers due to disillusionment with the Congress over its 'appeasement' of Muslims by 'conceding' the demand of Pakistan. For instance, Vishwa Nath Singh, lawyer from Lakhimpur Kheri in UP, wrote 'on behalf of the Hindu public of this Town' to enquire from the Congress president Kripalani why the Congress was making plans for celebrations. 'It is announced that 15 August is to be celebrated as a day of great national rejoicing,' he enquired. 'For what should we celebrate? The mother is cut into two and we are asked to rejoice over it,' he protested. In his view, it 'should be celebrated as a day of great mourning by the Hindus for it was a day of great shame and humiliation'.[43]

Throughout late July 1947, as the celebration plans evolved, the campaign to oppose them also gathered momentum. Its high point was the All India Hindu Convention organized in Delhi on 10 August, the week the celebrations were to commence. Presiding over the convention, Savarkar declared that 'Hindus could not rejoice in the coming Independence because it meant the establishment of Pakistan over one third of India and because untold suffering had been caused to millions of people by the orgy of plunder, arson, murder and conversion' which are likely to result from this policy of 'appeasement'. Nearly a dozen other speakers at the convention lent support to the demand that India should declare itself a Hindu state and work for Hindu ideals. Savarkar appealed to 'the Hindus irrespective of party affiliations to unite together, look ahead and be ready to face the dangers of partition'. He pointed out that:

> the Muslims had already begun to make further claims for a Moplastan, a Moestan and other 'stans'; they are also claiming separate districts for themselves in the Hindustan provinces; the Muslim princes are also threatening to establish Pakistans in their own territories; if these threats are not met there will be at least fourteen more Pakistans in the country in the next few years.

The only remedy, according to Savarkar, lay in rejecting the vivisection of 'Mother India', and the boycott of the celebrations was an integral part of this programme.[44]

While open boycott of the celebrations was just one form in which the Hindu right wing expressed itself, its campaign of pursuing its agenda of Hindutva also took the form of exerting pressure upon Congress which was now taking control of the state. Pressure was exerted, for instance, to get Devanagari official status as 'the *lingua franca* of India'.[45] Further, the suggestion was made to change the country's nomenclature from India to 'Hindustan'. As a Hindu right wing supporter demanded to know from Kripalani, 'You have requested the British to let the name India remain in place of Hindustan. What did you gain by this? You may profess anything, but India is no more India and it is divided and cut into two.'[46] It was demanded that India should declare itself a Hindu state, just as Pakistan was now being established in the name of Islam.[47]

A specific issue which Hindu nationalists took up on this occasion was their long-standing demand of a ban on cow slaughter. They mounted an extremely forceful and broad-based campaign to put pressure on Congress leaders to declare on 15 August that cow slaughter would be banned in free India. Hanuman Prasad Poddar, proprietor of the Gita Press and editor of *Kalyan*, a Hindi journal devoted to popularizing Hinduism, called upon Congress leaders to inaugurate the dominion by undertaking the first act of banning cow slaughter, 'now that the British are quitting our land and we are soon going to have a national government of our own'. He claimed that the demand had the sympathy of influential Congress leaders like Rajendra Prasad and even Gandhi.[48] The advocates of cow protection convened the All-India Anti-Cow Slaughter Conference in Delhi which demanded that the Indian Government accept 'protection, preservation and improvement of cow' as a fundamental right of the people.[49] So effective was the campaign that Rajendra Prasad, president of the CA, was reported to have received about 50,000 postcards, 30,000 letters and thousands of telegrams demanding the prohibition of cow slaughter in the Union of India. Gandhi himself was forced to respond to the issue; he reasoned that it was not possible to concede the demand, as 'Hindu religions prohibited cow slaughter for the Hindus, not for the world.' Thus, it could not become a matter of state policy. In his view 'religious prohibition came from within' and 'any imposition from without meant compulsion'. Further, Gandhi reasoned that

India was the land not only of the Hindus, but also of the Muslims, the Sikhs, the Parsis, the Christians, the Jews and [all those] who claimed to be of India and were loyal to the Union. If they could prohibit cow slaughter in India on religious grounds, why could not the Pakistan Government prohibit, say, idol worship in Pakistan on similar grounds?[50]

Gandhi's strong stance on this issue thus ensured that the demand for a ban on cow slaughter did not gather support.

The opposition to the idea of celebrations was not confined to the Hindu nationalists alone. A groundswell of opinion seemed to be building up which questioned the plans being made for the celebrations. A correspondent of Gandhi, a non-Muslim from a West Punjab district, captured the mood when he wrote in a letter to the Mahatma:

You people are talking loud about the celebration of Aug. 15 next as independence day. Have you thought how we the non-Muslims of Pakistan are to celebrate the day and with what joy in our hearts? We here shall be afraid about our own safety when you might be rejoicing. Can you direct us as to what we might do? Can it be a day of anything but mourning. Our Muslims neighbours have begun to put fright into out hearts from now.

What the Muslims of Indian union are thinking? Are they not likely to share the same fright? We are frightened to such an extent that we feel we are in danger of compulsory conversions to Islam. It is all very well for you to preach courage and to prattle that everyone's religion is his own keeping. It may be true of sanyasis, not of pure householders having children.[51]

Gandhi himself lent his weight to such expressions of doubt by declaring: 'This much I certainly believe that coming August 15 should be no day for rejoicing whilst the minorities contemplate the day with a heavy heart. It must be a day for prayer and deep heart-searching.' In his view there could be no rejoicing if the 'minorities' felt insecure and unprotected.[52] In Lucknow, the influential Muslim League leader Begum Aizaz Rasul openly expressed her apprehensions at the state of affairs. She expressly declared:

> There can be no peace in this vast subcontinent unless minorities are safeguarded in both dominions. . . . I feel that no assurances, whatsoever, are forthcoming for the Muslims of the Indian Union, though they have a legitimate and reasonable claim for the safeguard and protection of their cultural, social, political, religious and other rights. . . . This state of affairs will lead to insecurity and frustration, resulting in an anarchic situation for millions of people inhabiting the two Dominions who want to be good citizens of the new States'.[53]

In Calcutta, Haji Seth Mohammed Yusuf, a member of the Bengal Legislative Council and councillor of the Calcutta Corporation, painted a 'grim outlook' for Muslims in West Bengal as their future looked 'dark and gloomy'. He complained that no assurances had been given to Muslims about the 'safety and security of their lives, liberties, religion and culture'. He feared that 'on and from August 15th there will be a Hindu rule in West Bengal with a vengeance'. He could see that 'ominous signs are already appearing'; experience of the Great Calcutta Killings of 1946 had convinced him that 'August has not turned out in the past to be a very August month'.[54]

Similar sentiments of apprehension and anxiety

were being expressed by Hindus and Sikhs in Sind, West Punjab and the North Western Frontier Province (NWFP). So powerful was the mood against the proposed celebrations that even Kripalani was moved to declare:

> We know that the hearts of all Congressmen and Congress sympathisers in Sind, East Bengal, West Punjab and the NWFP are lacerated at the division of the country. They are therefore in no mood to rejoice with the rest of India. Under the circumstances, there is no need to celebrate August 15 in the areas which have been separated from India.

He directed the secretary of the Punjab Congress Committee to instruct local Congress committees in West Punjab not to join in the celebrations. A strong protest was made by Liaquat Ali Khan over the Congress president's statement; Muslim League workers complained that he was undermining the celebrations being planned for the inauguration of Pakistan by calling for a boycott. However, Kripalani refused to withdraw his call, although the Punjab Congress circular was withdrawn. He insisted that 'all those who feel the glow of a free Pakistan must participate in its celebrations. But for those who feel no such glow and are not happy over the division of the country, to participate in the celebrations would be an act of hypocrisy dictated by self-interest'.[55]

The Dravida Boycott

Meanwhile, in southern India, largely unaffected by the north's divisive politics of separatism and Partition, a different controversy was brewing. At its centre was E.V. Ramaswamy Naicker 'Periyar' (1879–1973), the iconoclastic leader of the Dravida movement. For over two decades, Periyar had singularly devoted his energies towards forging a Dravida political identity and sustaining a movement against brahmanical dominance, which he believed to be deeply entrenched in education, politics, government and sociocultural arenas in the Tamil-speaking parts of southern India. He regarded the Dravida people as indigenous to Tamil Nadu, in contrast to the brahmins whose ancestors were seen as Aryan invaders. His efforts had culminated in the setting in 1944 of the Dravida Kazagham (DK), a political party aiming at the removal of untouchability, promotion of women's rights, opposition to the imposition of Hindi and encouragement of rationalist thinking.

A powerful, 'saintly looking' orator with a white flowing beard, Periyar had no qualms in openly attacking the brahmins, whom he regarded as 'invaders from the north' who have 'twisted and perverted the religion and culture' of the Dravidians. He frequently poured scorn on the Congress as representing the Aryan culture of the north and denounced Gandhi as a 'traitor and cheat'. In 1938 he had raised the demand for a separate 'Dravidistan' or 'Dravida Nadu' ('Land of the Dravidas') much before Jinnah raised the banner for a separate Muslim nation. Over time, Periyar extended the idea of Dravida Nadu to include the Telugu, Malayalam and Kannada speaking parts of the Madras Presidency.[56]

Even as Independence approached, the DK issued a statement on 25 July 1947 terming the designated day as a 'day of mourning'.[57] Two days later Periyar described the approaching 15 August as a 'British Bania-Brahmin Contractual Day', calling it a 'dark day' because Independence was 'incomplete' without Dravida empowerment and as the goal of Dravida Nadu remained unfulfilled.[58] On 6 August 1947 another statement urged Dravidians to assemble and hold meetings to reiterate the idea of separation, while exhorting them not to participate in the 15 August celebrations.

While Periyar's views defined the DK's stand, his lieutenant C.N. Annadurai and secretary of the party, in a shrewd and significant move, distanced himself from this condemnation. In a lengthy statement issued on 10 August 1947, Annadurai defied his mentor, calling 15 August 'historic' and an event that had caught the 'interest of the entire world'. Annadurai went on to argue: 'August 15 is a day when the 200 years of blame and shame of the continent is about to be wiped. It is a festive day for the Dravidians too—not a day of mourning', calling it a day when 'one of the two enemies was done with (what remains is Bania imperialism)'.[59]

While Periyar's views defined the DK's stance, the younger generation of Tamils attracted to Dravida ideology, felt closer to Annadurai's position. In fact, at many places, Dravida activists, who hoisted black flags and wore black shirts to mourn the day, had to face the hostility of people at large. In Cuddalore and Tirunelveli, Dravida cadres had to face violent attacks, recalled K. Veeramani, the present head of the DK.[60]

However, notwithstanding the Dravida boycott,

many oral-history accounts highlight the sense of elation and festivity with which the occasion was celebrated. S. Pandian, then a high school student in Madras, recalled that 'every street corner was festooned with flags be it in khadi, silk or paper . . . women prepared sweet pongal in temples and drew special kolams outside their houses'. The Madras premier O. Ramaswamy Reddiar presided over the official celebrations. Across the Madras Presidency, radio sets were installed in parks for the public to listen to the All India Radio broadcast of the midnight ceremony in New Delhi. Patriotic songs were played in the streets while theatres in Madras city threw open their doors for free shows.

Naga Declaration of 'Independence'

Meanwhile, the north-eastern region, seen as distant and inaccessible from the northern part of India, saw startling political stirrings in the run up to 15 August 1947. In Assam's Sylhet district, a fiercely contested political battle was waged between the 'Axe' and the 'Hut', symbols used in a referendum held on 6 July 1947 to decide its fate. The 'Axe' symbolized a vote to join East Pakistan and the 'Hut' the vote to remain in Assam, a part of India. Notwithstanding the verdict of the referendum, Sylhet also came up for 'dissection' before the Radcliffe Boundary Commission and its fate was revealed only on 17 August 1947.[61]

In another corner of the North-East, the Chittagong Hill Tracts (CHT), a group of districts which had been a part of the Chittagong division of East Bengal, concerns existed about the future. Even though non-Muslims communities made up 68 per cent of the CHT's demography and Muslims constituted a minority at 24 per cent, the region were awarded to East Pakistan.

A number of tribes which inhabited the north-eastern region—most notably the Naga and the Zo communities—were 'trans-national' as their footprint spread beyond colonial Assam to East Bengal, Burma and China.[62] Under colonial rule, the British had conveniently used the province of Assam as a 'hold-all' for the very diverse communities, regions and subregions that make up the present day states of north-eastern India.

The Nagas approached the coming of Independence with a deep sense of anxiety about their own future. The end of World War II and the looming British departure led to stirrings among the Nagas, worried about safeguarding their land, culture and way of life. The Naga National Council in the months preceding August 1947 held a series of consultations with the governor of Assam and with the Congress leadership in New Delhi; they even reached out to Mahatma Gandhi and Jawaharlal Nehru. However, the Naga leadership itself did not speak in one voice. While the moderate elements were content with assurances of autonomy within India, the hardliners, led by Angami Zapu Phizo (1913–90) openly spoke of 'independence' for the Nagas.[63]

The diaries of Mildred Archer, art historian and wife of W.G. Archer of the ICS who then served in the Naga Hills, provide an 'odd and unusual angle' on the events as they were unfolding. She noted: 'For most of India 15 August was a day of rejoicing, of freedom from a hated foreign domination, but in the Naga Hills it was a day of consternation for there British rule was still respected while Indians were suspected and disliked.'[64]

In a dramatic move, the People's Independence League, a faction of the Naga National Council led by Phizo, met in Kohima. It gave a call to the Nagas to boycott the Independence Day celebrations and, on 14 August 1947, it declared the independence of the Naga region.[65] A telegram was drafted to the United Nations which read: 'Benign excellence, kindly put on record that Nagas will be independent. Discussion with India are being carried on to that effect. Nagas do not accept Indian Constitution. The right of the people must prevail regardless of size.'[66]

In its immediate context, the declaration proved to be a non-event. 'Since 15 August, nothing has happened', Archer noted in her diary, as nothing was done 'to set up a rival government. . . . having declared their independence they are now at loss to know what to do next'.[67] Nonetheless, the 14 August 1947 declaration remains 'a fact of significance in narratives of Naga nationhood', especially in the context of the armed insurgency which engulfed the Nagas in subsequent decades.

The Consecration Rituals in Karachi

Notwithstanding such doubts and apprehensions, the curtain on the actual ceremonics marking the British withdrawal from the subcontinent was raised on 14

August in Karachi, the newly designated capital of Pakistan. For Muslims celebrating the foundation of Pakistan, the day could not have been better chosen. As Nawabzada Liaquat Ali Khan, the prime minister designate, declared:

> Our National State will be inaugurated on a very auspicious day, namely, Jumat-ul-Wida or the last Friday in Ramazan. Therefore the Muslims will have the opportunity of observing the best of all celebrations—offering special prayers after the Jumma prayers, invoking the blessings of God for Pakistan and soliciting Divine grace for all its citizens so that they may prove worthy of the great future which is now theirs.[68]

Many devout Muslims saw it as a particularly propitious beginning for the 'Land of the Pure',

In areas expected to become a part of Pakistan all attention had been centred on Karachi, the capital designate, where the ceremonies connected with the transfer of power were to be staged. The city had begun feverish preparations for the historic role it was now being called upon to play, 'the greatest moment in the Muslim nation's history for the past 200 years' as the *Dawn* described it.[69]

In July 1947, a special committee steered by the top personnel of the Sind provincial government and fully backed by its administrative machinery had been formed to draw up suitable plans for the celebrations. This committee had decided that the entire city was to be decorated with flags and buntings; buildings were to be illuminated and sweets distributed in schools. Even a release of prisoners was contemplated as part of the celebrations.[70] A citizens' committee, chaired by the president of the Sind Muslim League, Yusuf Haroon, had also been formed. Suggestions had poured in and plans were made to create an atmosphere of 'gaiety and solemnity' on that very special day. Efforts had been made to associate the leaders of non-Muslim communities with the work of the committee; the response, on their part, was encouraging. The Sind Congress leadership, represented by N.R. Malkani and Mukhi Govind Ram, joined the committee and issued an appeal urging all non-Muslims in Sind to participate in the celebrations. 'There must be no sorrowful heart nor hungry mouth on those festive days', they declared.[71] The organizers reported 'phenomenal success' in getting donations from commercial firms, with an 'appreciable predominance of non-Muslims'. The Dalmia Cement Company, for instance, gave Rs.5,000 and a similar amount was presented by Tara Chand Gupta of the Iron and Steel Merchants' Association. There were even suggestions that Muslims were complaining that they were 'not having enough say' in the work of the committee.[72]

For the residents of Karachi, the new occupant of the Government House was a very special person. The celebrations also marked the homecoming of the city's greatest son, Muhammed Ali Jinnah. His return to the city of his birth, according to *Dawn*, was the end of a journey from a 'cradle room in a nursery to the throne room of the Governor-General's House in the selfsame city' which had 'no parallel in modern history'.[73] Karachi eagerly awaited the return of its greatest son in 'his supreme moment of glory'. The raging popularity of the *Quaid-i-Azam* was evident from the varied types of Jinnah caps which were selling like hot cakes, spoiling the buyers with choice: there was 'Jinnah Popular' made of 'imitation fur' available for Rs.2; then 'Jinnah Jafar' made with 'plush and allied materials' which sold for Rs.10; 'Jinnah Standard' made of 'Indian fur' for the more discerning clientele, which sold for Rs.45; and finally, the top of the range 'Jinnah Special' made with the choicest 'Qaraquri fur' priced at Rs.75.[74]

On 5 August 1947 an advanced party consisting of Lt. S.M. Ahsan and Capt. Gul Hassan Khan, ADCs to the Governor General designate, arrived together with Major McCoy, who was to take charge as comptroller at the Government House. Within two days arrangements

Plate 1: Jinnah's arrival at Karachi Airport, 7 August 1947 (courtesy Nazaria-i-Pakistan Trust)

were in place for the arrival of the *Quaid* himself. On 7 August, Jinnah, accompanied by his sister Fatima, flew in from Delhi in the Viceroy's personal Dakota. Wearing a cream-colored silk *sherwani*, a *shalwar* and his trademark fur cap, Jinnah was received by the members designate of the Pakistan cabinet, the Sind premier, the mayor of Karachi and a Citizens' Reception Committee.[75] Also present were representatives of the Sind Minorities' Association who wished to present a memorandum enumerating their demands to the 'supreme leader' of Pakistan. The enthusiastic crowd of more than 50,000 which had gathered at the Mauripur airfield surged through police cordons when the plane landed, many hoping to catch a glimpse of Jinnah.[76] To mark the 'homecoming', the Sind Government declared a public holiday on that day. Hundreds of cars formed a 3 mi. procession as Jinnah drove through the streets of Karachi. The homecoming was emotional for Jinnah too. He was presented a Guard of Honour and was attended by attendants dressed in scarlet. Upon entering Government House, he was said to have remarked to his ADC, 'Do you know I never expected to see Pakistan in my lifetime. We have to be grateful to Almighty God for this great gift.'[77] For the city the celebrations had already begun.

On 10 August Jinnah attended the first public function which was the inauguration of the Pakistan Constituent Assembly. Feverish preparations had been underway at the Secretariat to put finishing touches to the refitting of the chamber, previously used by the Sind Legislative Assembly. At what was described as 'a simple and dignified' ceremony, the Pakistan Constituent Assembly held its inaugural session where it elected Jogendranath Mandal, a prominent non-Muslim leader from East Bengal, as its temporary chairman. Calling it 'a momentous occasion', Mandal welcomed all those who had come from different parts of Pakistan to Karachi. These included the premiers of Muslim-majority states like Qazi Nazimuddin of East Bengal as well as important non-Muslim leaders like Lala Bhimsen Sachar, leader of the West Punjab Congress, and Kiron Shankar Roy, a Congress leader from East Bengal. Mandal called upon all citizens, especially from the 'minorities', to be 'responsible, loyal and faithful to the State'. Loud cheers filled the chamber when he came forward to sign the roll as a founder-member of the Pakistan Constituent Assembly. There was much applause again when Kiron Shankar Roy presented his credentials and signed the roll. In all, the assembly had sixty-nine members, made up of fifty Muslim representatives and seventeen Hindu and two Sikh members.[78]

The following day the *Quaid* himself addressed the Assembly. In his first speech as leader of Pakistan, Jinnah began by defining his priority 'to maintain law and order so that the life, property and religious beliefs of its subjects are fully protected by the State'. Jinnah was only too aware that the state which he had worked so hard to achieve, though created in acrimonious and unhappy circumstances, should not at its birth be sullied by lingering communal distrust and antagonism. He then went on to warn against 'curses' which the new nation must guard against: bribery, corruption, black marketing, nepotism and jobbery. Such evils must not be tolerated and should be 'put down with an iron hand'. He urged his countrymen to strive together:

> Now, if we want to make this great State of Pakistan happy and prosperous we should wholly and solely concentrate on the well-being of the people, and especially of the masses and the poor. If you will work in co-operation, forgetting the past, burying the hatchet, you are bound to succeed. If you change your past and work together in a spirit that every one of you, no matter what community he belongs, no matter what relations he had with you in the past, no matter what is his colour, caste, or creed, is first, second and last a citizen of this State with equal rights, privileges, and obligations, there will be no end to the progress you will make.

He then went on to declare: 'I cannot emphasise it too much. We should begin to work in that spirit and in course of time all these angularities of the majority and "minority" communities, the Hindu community and the Muslim community . . . will vanish.' Then he came to 'the core of his speech . . . his credo'. He told the citizens of Pakistan in 'a characteristically vigorous fashion':

> You are free; you are free to go to your temples, you are free to go to your mosques or to any other place of worship in this State of Pakistan. . . . You may belong to any religion or caste or creed—that has nothing to do with the business of the State. . . . We are starting in the days when there is no discrimination, no distinction between one community and another, no discrimination between one caste or creed and another. We are starting with this fundamental principle that we are all citizens of one State.

In retrospect, these words spoken by the 'Founder of the Nation' at the inauguration of the Pakistan Constituent Assembly seem ironic. Did Jinnah really mean that religion did not matter as far as matters of State were concerned? Then, what was the 'Land of the Pure' all about? Chaudhury Mohammad Ali in his *The Emergence of Pakistan* speculates:

> Could it be . . . that as soon as Pakistan was won the *Quaid-i-Azam* abandoned the two-nation theory and invited all its citizens, Muslims and non-Muslims alike, to work together for the state on the basis of territorial nationalism? What then was its *raison d'etre,* and what would be its distinguishing characteristics? Had the two nation theory merely been the scaffolding that was to be discarded once the structure was built?

Jinnah's speech has been interpreted by scholars in several different ways. Mohammad Ali believes that:

> what is overlooked is that Pakistan came into existence not by conquest but as a result of a negotiated agreement between the representatives of the Hindu and Muslim communities to partition the subcontinent. An explicit and integral part of the agreement was that minorities in both states would have equal rights and equal protection of law. In that context the Quaid-i-Azam was wholly right in asserting the fundamental principle that 'we are all citizens and equal citizens of one State'.[79]

For instance, Stanley Wolpert, a biographer of Jinnah, seems confounded when he writes in astonishment at the words uttered by his protagonist:

> What was he talking about? Had he simply forgotten where he was? Had the cyclone of events so disoriented him that

he was arguing the opposition's brief? Was he pleading for a united India—on the eve of Pakistan—before those hundreds of thousands of terrified innocents were slaughtered, fleeing their homes, their fields, their ancestral villages and running to an eternity of oblivion or a refugee camp in a strange land?[80]

However, several Pakistani scholars believe that Jinnah's inaugural Constituent Assembly speech represented what he really stood for—his 'creed'—which has been suppressed by ruling vested interests, so much so that 'a distorted, censored version' was supplied to Jinnah's official biographer, Hector Bolitho, for a book commissioned by the Government of Pakistan.[81] The Pakistani scholar Akbar Ahmed has called this speech Jinnah's 'Gettysburg Address'. According to him it was 'an outpouring of ideas on the state and nature of society, almost a stream of consciousness' which reflected the *Quaid*'s 'vision for the state he had created'.[82]

Likewise, the historian Ayesha Jalal has noted that, 'although the speech was promptly suppressed by the official guardians of Pakistan's ideological frontiers, it has served as the *magna carta* for those who . . . style themselves as the true inheritors of Jinnah's political legacy'.[83] Jinnah's words seem ironic in view of the direction which Pakistan's polity has taken in the seventy-five years of its post-Independence history. However, when they were spoken, Jinnah's declaration revealed his vision of the new nation in which he envisaged an equal place for all citizens, irrespective of religion or creed.

Meanwhile, Karachi continued its feverish preparations for the big day. Unlike the imperial capital New Delhi, the city of Karachi hardly had the physical wherewithal or the necessary political resources to assume the role which it was being called upon to play. Even as preparations were under way to mark Pakistan's birth, a government was literally being created overnight in Karachi. Here was a capital city with hardly any government offices, ministries, office furniture or stationery. Typewriters were regarded as a luxury and, in administrative terms, the situation was described as utterly chaotic.[84]

Nonetheless, there was enthusiasm in welcoming the birth of Pakistan. The *Dawn* reported that 'Karachi swarms with pioneers picnicking, with an air of excitement'. The 'Pakistan Specials' brought civil servants from India daily, and were full of people who 'alight in the promised land with vociferous cheer'. The administrative machinery of the new state was slowly taking shape. 'Cabinet Ministers of Pakistan use packing cases as desks and crack jokes with painters who drip whitewash on them' and it was reported that even Government House did not possess a telephone directory![85]

When Wilfred Russell, representative of the British firm Killick Nixon and Company, visited the prime minister's house to discuss with him the feasibility of acquiring a fast, long-range Royal Viking aircraft for Jinnah, he found that 'workmen were swarming all over the house unpacking, painting, hanging up curtains and scrubbing floors'. It all seemed quite 'typical of the pioneering atmosphere of Karachi at that time'.[86]

Meanwhile, those expected to arrive for the transfer-of-power ceremonies had begun their journey to Karachi. General Auchinleck, the British army chief and his military secretary, Shahid Hamid, on their way from Delhi, flew over East Punjab and came in very low to watch the columns of refugees proceeding to Pakistan. Hamid recalls, 'We saw areas in smoke that were burning. They were obviously Muslim. Smoke covered the countryside. It presented a grim picture of a battleground.' At Lahore they had met the West Punjab Governor Evan Jenkins, General Peter Rees of the newly formed Punjab Boundary Force and Colonel Ayub Khan who 'did not mince their words and painted a very gloomy picture'. They were told that the Sikhs were behaving with 'pre-medieval ferocity' and felt that the worst was still to come. Hamid arrived in Karachi 'thoroughly depressed after witnessing the carnage of the Muslims which was taking place in East Punjab'. He 'immediately went to the *Quaid* and Liaquat and told them of the happenings and the gruesome sights' he had witnessed.[87]

Not unexpectedly, within Karachi the 'minorities' were growing increasingly apprehensive. Russell could observe in the streets that 'the considerable numbers of Hindus who had lived there peacefully side by side with the Muslims for generations, were obviously a bit worried and were beginning to look over their shoulders into India'. The enthusiastic contributions by non-Muslim business groups reflected a certain nervousness, an attempt by propertied groups to secure goodwill in an environment which could suddenly become hostile. On 12 August 1947, Sri Prakasa, a prominent

Congress leader from UP and a personal friend of Nehru, arrived in Karachi to take charge as India's first high commissioner.[88] Within a few hours he was met by Choithram Gidwani, the most prominent Congress leader of Sind. Sri Prakasa, who found the latter 'in an angry mood', recalls:

> [He] asked me what I meant by being there at all? He told me that he had been the President of the Provincial Congress Committee continuously for twenty-five years; and when he was available for the job, no body [*sic*] had any business to come. I must confess I was taken aback; and I told him as quietly as I could, that I was not responsible for my presence, and that he should go to the Prime Minister to know why I should have been sent.[89]

Quite clearly, both men had little idea of the nature of bilateral ties which the two dominions were expected to establish. It was interesting that Gidwani, who was undoubtedly the most prominent non-Muslim politician in Sind, viewed himself not as a citizen of Pakistan but as someone who naturally should be the diplomatic representative of India in the capital of Pakistan! When Sri Prakasa invited him to celebrations which he had organized at the Palace Hotel to mark Indian Independence, Gidwani refused to attend the function. 'He said he was too upset to come to any such functions for freedom, for freedom was not real freedom for which Sind had been sacrificed.'[90]

On the evening of 13 August 1947, Mountbatten and his party flew in from Delhi and were immediately driven to Government House for a banquet where 'pleasant, mutually complimentary and felicitous

Plate 2: Mountbatten at the Constituent Assembly of Pakistan session in Karachi, 14 August 1947 (courtesy Nazaria-i-Pakistan Trust)

speeches were delivered by Lord Mountbatten and Mr. Jinnah'. This was followed by an outdoor reception. To Alan Campbell-Johnson, Jinnah 'the host and hero of the occasion', appeared to his guests like 'an aloof, almost lonely figure . . . at this historic moment'. Hamid, also present at the reception, found him 'quiet and aloof, but he felt proud of such a leader. He looked

Plate 3: Jinnah addressing the Constituent Assembly, 14 August 1947 (courtesy Nazaria-i-Pakistan Trust)

every inch the Father of the Nation and the Founder of the ideological State of Pakistan', he later recalled.

That night, at one minute past midnight, as 14 August began, Radio Pakistan came on air to announce the birth of the new nation. A recitation from the Quran was followed by a hymn sung by Zafar Ali Khan: '*Quaid-i-Azam*, we are indebted to you'.[91] The next morning, Mountbatten and Jinnah were to ride through the streets of Karachi on their way to the Constituent Assembly. However, there had been intelligence reports warning of an impending bomb attack on their motorcade.[92] Jinnah had been alerted to the danger and the suggestion was made that they should either cancel the journey or at least go in a closed car instead of an open Rolls Royce. However, both disregarded these

Plate 4: Fatima and Mohammad Ali Jinnah and Louis and Edwina Mountbatten in Karachi (courtesy Nazaria-i-Pakistan Trust)

reports as alarmist fears and decided to go ahead.[93] The proceedings were carried out according to plans. Right on schedule Jinnah arrived in a state landau and inspected the troops, drawn up in a large hollow square, under the command of their respective British commanding officers. A stately and dignified Jinnah led observers to comment that 'he could have given points in dignity and deportment to the most stately of British Viceroys'.[94] 'A squadron of Tempests roared in salute' and the parade was 'carried out with a precision and smartness which augured well for the future'. After the inspection of troops, Jinnah, undaunted by the bomb threat, proceeded in an open car to the Constituent Assembly with Mountbatten. Gerry O'Neill, a soldier on duty in Karachi during the parade, witnessed the motorcade:

In the lead car were Mountbatten, looking every bit the '*El Supremo*' in his naval uniform, with about one square foot of medals and Jinnah. Behind them were Fatimah Jinnah and Edwina Mountbatten. . . . Mohammed Ali Jinnah was . . . completely at ease and obviously enjoying himself, but not gloating in his role as the new Governor General. His thin,

Plate 5: Mountbatten and Jinnah at the Constituent Assembly
(courtesy Nazaria-i-Pakistan Trust)

aquiline features were not fixed in a smile, but showed emotion and concern for the occasion.[95]

In the assembly, the ceremony marking the birth of Pakistan was short and dignified. Mountbatten read out the King's Message. He then went on to express the hope that the minorities in Pakistan would enjoy equal rights as citizens and offered the example of the Mughal Emperor Akbar as a model for the new state. However, according to Ahmed, this suggestion was particularly inappropriate as 'for many Muslims Akbar posed many problems'.[96] 'To propose Akbar as an ideal ruler to a newly formed and self-consciously post-colonial Muslim nation', comments Ahmed, 'was rather like suggesting to a convention of Muslim writers meeting in Iran or Pakistan that their literary model should be Salman Rushdie'.[97] A reply from Jinnah followed in which he reiterated that the tradition of tolerance and goodwill among the Muslims went back to the days of the Prophet himself, rather than the much later example of Akbar. The short ceremony, lasting less than an hour, ended with everyone congratulating each other.[98] Jinnah and Mountbatten then went out in procession to Government House. Enthusiastic spectators lined the streets. Though the bomb threat never materialized, the old Rolls Royce which carried the dignitaries, borrowed from the ruler of a state, caught fire as soon as the occupants disembarked as its engine had overheated.[99] Relieved that they had made the procession unscathed, Jinnah was said to have turned to Mountbatten and said, 'Thank goodness I have brought you back safely.'

Outside the Governor's House and the Constituent

Plate 6: Jinnah taking the oath as Governor General from Justice Mian Sir Abdul Rashid (courtesy Nazaria-i-Pakistan Trust)

Assembly, the festive mood in Karachi was deceptive.[100] Campbell-Johnson, private secretary to Mountbatten, noted, while passing along the official route, that 'neither the scale nor the enthusiasm of the crowds was anything like as great as I had expected . . . the greetings of the crowd, apart from some lorry loads of hilarious soldiers from the Pakistan Navy and the usual excitement of children, were decorous rather than ecstatic'.[101]

The atmosphere was not 'terribly demonstrative,

Plate 7: Jinnah after taking oath as Governor General of Pakistan
(courtesy Nazaria-i-Pakistan Trust)

Plate 8: Liaquat Ali Khan after swearing in as Prime Minister
(courtesy Nazaria-i-Pakistan Trust)

Plate 9: Jinnah with Liaquat Ali Khan and his Cabinet (courtesy Nazaria-i-Pakistan Trust)

rather "provincial" and "sober", but not ecstatic as in India'.[102] On the other hand, Hamid recalls that 'all along the route there was great enthusiasm and wild cheering. . . . A dream was coming true and a State was being born. The name of Quaid-e-Azam was on everyone's lips as well as their thanks to the Almighty'. Russell, then lodged in the Palace Hotel which was crammed with press people, decided to be out in the streets to 'squeeze every drop of experience out of this great day'.[103] The mood of Independence was certainly there, as witnessed by the new green and white Pakistan flags that were sprouting from rooftops, balconies and windows. However, he sensed that most of the 'ordinary people in the street had scarcely realised that Pakistan had really come about'. While everyone knew that the challenges facing the new state were immense, the spirit

Plate 10: Fatima and M.A. Jinnah arriving at Karachi Club on the evening of 14 August 1947 (courtesy Nazaria-i-Pakistan Trust)

of 14 August was one of goodwill. Russell had a sense of that as he observed the celebrations in Karachi:

> Sitting on an old Ford surrounded by a cross-section of Indian Muslims, all restrained, yet fervently happy, as far as I could tell, I felt the tears coming to my eyes. It was all so sensible and friendly with real comradeship between the new and the old, real understanding on both sides. Pray God it will last.[104]

In the evening, after Mountbatten and his party had left, the Karachi Club hosted a 'grand independence banquet' where the city's *crème de la crème* jostled to felicitate the *Quaid-i-Azam*. The club had been established in 1934 by the elite Hindu Amil community, mostly from Shikarpur, the Bohri Muslim community and old, titled Sindhi families. Ken Mac, the well-known musician and conductor who performed at the Cricket Club of India in Bombay, had been flown by a special Tata airlines plane to perform at this event. Jinnah arrived with his sister Fatima for the banquet and was received by the club's president Justice Tyabji and its honorary secretary Jethanand Tandon. They were led to the other guests which included cabinet members, the diplomatic corps, the Commander-in-Chief Sir Douglas Gracey, British civilian and army officers and Pakistani officers like Iskander Mirza, all 'resplendent in cummerbunds or dress suits with the ladies in colourful sarees and evening dresses'. At the sit-down dinner around the teak dance floor, they were serenaded by Ken Mac and his band. Haji Bhai Esmail Dossa, a Bombay-based businessman, recalls the highlights of the evening:

> Sir Ghulam Hussain Hidayatullah requested Ken Mac to play 'So deep is the night' because on that Chopin tune, Ruttie had taken Jinnah's consent for marriage in the Taj Mahal ballroom, at her birthday party, on February 20th, 1918. Later, the Quaid requested the orchestra for Paul Robson's 'The End' which as a courtesy to the Quaid, was sung in the tenor voice, by the great Ken Mac himself, for it was known that the Founder used to hum the words of 'The End' on Thursday afternoons in Bombay that he devoted to visit the grave of his wife Ruttie, in the Khoja Isna'asheri cemetery of Bombay.
>
> The finale of the evening, was given to the music 'Happy Birthday Dina' because the Quaid had chosen the Independence Day of Pakistan, on the birthday of his only daughter Dina,

whom he had left behind in Bombay, with her two children Nusli and Diana. And when the programme ended the Quaid stood up, the guests followed, and everyone lifted their glasses, to toast 'God save the King'.[105]

While the music played to the August gathering, the mood was changing outside in the streets of Karachi, as news was coming in of the disturbances in Punjab and northern India. The ominous signs were evident for all to see. Campbell-Johnson, on his return flight to Delhi, noticed the 'large fires in the Punjab [as] beacons of ill omen dominating the landscapes for miles around'.[106] The uncertainties felt by the non-Muslims who had, for the moment, chosen to stay with the new state, tempered the mood of Independence in Karachi, as elsewhere in Pakistan. If, indeed, Pakistan marked the creation of a state for the Muslims, would there be a future in the new country for Hindus, Sikhs, Parsis and Christians?

Jinnah and his lieutenants had, of course, on every conceivable occasion sought to allay the fears of non-Muslim communities. The Independence Day Celebration Committee had made it a point to include 'minority' members. Constant reminders had been made by leaders that 'minorities' should 'be loyal to their respective states'. In an editorial published in the *Dawn* on 3 August, the newspaper had supported the call by Liaquat Ali, prime minister designate, to observe 15 August as a 'day of deliverance' from foreign subjugation. But the underlying message was for all peoples of the new state to honour their new countries, and not let the 'newly acquired freedom be threatened by violence and blood'. Jinnah's speech on 11 August was the firmest indication yet of Pakistan's commitment to honour the rights and freedom of all its citizens, regardless of their religious beliefs.

Thus, the mood in Karachi on 14 August, as the British withdrew from the subcontinent, was ambivalent. For the Muslims, it was a time for rejoicing as the birth of Pakistan marked freedom and the creation of a separate state in the name of Islam. Reactions from non-Muslims were more guarded; they were unsure if the new state would deprive them of their rights. For the moment, they could seek solace in Jinnah's promise that their rights as 'minorities' in the new state were assured. This feeling was reinforced the following day, when Jinnah attended a Dominion Day service held in Karachi's Anglican Cathedral. In Karachi, at 'the first bright dawn of independence', the peace that freedom promised seemed, for the moment at least, to have become a reality.

'It Was a Lovely Time to Walk in Delhi'

Meanwhile, the capital city of Delhi had been gearing itself for the coming event which would make it the focus of world attention. Representatives of the press from all over the world had arrived to cover the transfer-of-power ceremonies and the BBC had sent its best equipment and camera teams for the occasion. In the Delhi Municipal Corporation (DMC), both Muslim League and Congress members had, in a rare show of unity, resolved to celebrate the occasion together. They had urged the citizens of Delhi to forget 'past bitterness and start a new era of mutual cooperation, communal harmony and a well-knit city life'.[107] Only one member of the Corporation, Ran Singh of the Hindu Mahasabha, had opposed the celebrations as, in his opinion, the motherland was being 'balkanized', and 15 August was a day 'not for rejoicing but of mourning'.[108] Elaborate plans had been made for sprucing up the city, arranging for free distribution of sweets and specially designed 'independence medals' inscribed with the national insignia on one side and '*Jai Hind!*' on the reverse to schoolchildren.[109]

While these feverish preparations were being made, the Muslim League, for its part, had made special efforts to avoid any controversy. Several of its leaders had repeatedly called upon the city's Muslim residents to come forward and join the celebrations.[110] Other political groups too had been forthcoming in wanting to participate. For instance, the Communists, bitter opponents of the Congress since the Quit India Movement of 1942, had issued an appeal to the 'followers of the Red Flag, all sections of the organized working class and other sections of the people' to join the celebrations.[111]

While there was no Muslim opposition to the proposed celebrations, there had been obvious concerns about the place of Muslims in them. There had also been growing concerns about the safety of the community. Activities of extreme communal organizations, the shifting of key officials in the city's law-and-order machinery, and news of violence against the Meos in the bordering south-western districts had caused much fright among the 'minority' community. In the last week of July, the Delhi Muslim League had been moved to appeal for funds for the relief of Muslims who had suffered. It was reported that 150 Muslim villages in Gurgaon district and over 160 Muslim villages in the princely state of Bharatpur had been burnt to ashes and, as a result, almost 25,000 Muslims had been rendered homeless.[112] A large number of these had evacuated to Delhi and were living in temporary shelters on pavements. They offered a sharp contrast to the decorations and arches put up by Congress volunteers, municipal authorities and young enthusiasts. In the prevailing circumstances, the question of celebrations had become a problematic one from the point of view of Delhi's Muslim residents. While their leaders never seriously contemplated the question of boycott—such a move would have invited hostility and even imperilled the safety of the community—there is considerable evidence to suggest that they now awaited the event with anxiety, if not apprehension.

Let us now turn our attention to Vallabhbhai Patel, who was at the centre of the historic event which was unfolding. Patel spent much of 14 August 1947—'the last day in unfree India'—following his usual routine, beginning with a morning walk at 5 a.m. in the Lodhi Gardens, a discussion with Nehru and interviews and working sessions with his close aides, V.P. Menon (secretary in the newly created Department of States), V. Shankar of the ICS, his private secretary, and with other callers which included politicians, princes and officials. At 3 p.m. he attended a Congress party meeting in the

Constituent Assembly and thereafter at 7 p.m. he was at Nehru's residence at York Road for an informal meeting of the new Cabinet in which he was to be deputy prime minister, with the heavy responsibility of the Home, States and Information and Broadcasting portfolios. Rajmohan Gandhi, the Sardar's biographer notes:

> There was no space, in Patel's packed day, for any conscious reflection on loved ones and companions who had gone, or on the dream about to be fulfilled, or on the fires of hate illumining the emergence of free India, or on the greatness and wonder, nonetheless, of what was emerging. Vallabhbhai's eyes and ears took in the day's details, his mind ticked away and his tongue sallied and slashed, but there was no time to cup an ear against history. [113]

In preparation for the midnight session, he and his daughter Manibehn went to Rajendra Prasad's residence, where Hindu prayers had been organized in which many leaders, including Nehru, were present. By now enthusiastic crowds had filled up the entire Central Vista area and it took them over half an hour to reach the Constituent Assembly. There Patel heard the speeches of Sarvepalli Radhakrishnan, followed by Nehru's memorable 'Tryst-with-Destiny' address. Rajmohan Gandhi writes:

> All that Vallabhbhai did was to join the other members, at the midnight hour, in a pledge of service. No one else in the Assembly had played a greater role in the arrival of the hour, yet there is something apt about Patel making only a simple pledge on the occasion, his utterance lost in a multitude of voices and audible only to himself. . . . After the ceremony, the old warrior had trouble locating his car and driver. . . . Vallabhbhai reached

his bed, stretched his weary limbs and eased his head onto a pillow wrapped in khadi. Sleep may soon have come, but in the minutes or seconds until it did the agony and ecstasy of the past must have broken loose from his depths and, colliding with the miracle of the hour, flooded his tired eyes.[114]

On the evening of 14 August, a special function was arranged at Prasad's residence on Queen's Road 'to give a send-off in the traditional fashion by ladies of Delhi' to Nehru, other ministers and constitution-makers. From Tanjore came priests from the Pandarsannidhi of Thiruvadhurai Adhinam, a special order of Hindu ascetics, who brought 'holy water' which they sprinkled on the leaders. Prasad and Nehru sat around a holy fire amidst the chanting of hymns, and women marked their forehead with *mangal tilak* (holy vermilion). It was traditional in Hindu custom to derive power and authority from priests. Nehru yielded to such rituals under pressure from close associates who argued that this was the traditional method of assuming power. The leaders then proceeded to the Constituent Assembly.[115] By 10 p.m. huge crowds had assembled outside the building, inspite of a spell of monsoon showers which had failed to dampen their spirits. As the leaders arrived to enter the building, they roared in greeting.

At 11 p.m. the Constituent Assembly began its special midnight session which was chaired by Prasad. The chamber was filled with newly starched dhotis and 'Gandhi caps'. The front rows were occupied by Vallabhbhai Patel, Rajkumari Amrit Kaur and others. Also in the front row sat Maulana Abul Kalam Azad, the 'nationalist Muslim' leader whose 'sad face' appeared

Plate 11: 'Tilak' being put on Jawaharlal Nehru after a Hindu *havan* ceremony at Rajendra Prasad's residence on the night of 14 August 1947, before their departure for the midnight ceremony. To Nehru's left is Rajkumari Amrit Kaur (courtesy Photo Division, Ministry of Information and Broadcasting)

'something of a tragedy, sticking out from the sea of happy faces like a gaunt and ravaged rock'.[116] The proceedings commenced with the singing of 'Vande Mataram' by the prominent Congress leader Sucheta Kripalani who sang the first verse of the anthem. Thereupon, Prasad as president of the Assembly commenced his address in Hindi. He recalled the sacrifices of those who had toiled for freedom. He paid a glowing tribute to Mahatma Gandhi, 'our beacon light' who 'represents that undying spirit in our culture and make-up which has kept India alive through vicissitudes of our history'. He then acknowledged the deep sense of sorrow at the Partition of the country: 'The country, which was made by God

Plate 12: Rajendra Prasad, President of the Constituent Assembly, congratulating Mountbatten on his appointment to the Governor Generalship of the Dominion of India from 14 August 1947 (courtesy Photo Division, Ministry of Information and Broadcasting)

and Nature to be one, stands divided today. Separation from near and dear ones, even from strangers after some association, is always painful. I would be untrue to myself if I did not at this moment confess to a sense of sorrow at this separation.' He had a word of cheer for those 'on the other side of the border' whom he urged to 'stick to their hearths and homes'. To the 'minorities' of India he had a word of assurance that they would receive 'fair and just treatment' and enjoy 'full rights

Plate 13: Singing of nationalist songs during the midnight session on 14–15 August 1947 (courtesy Photo Division, Ministry of Information and Broadcasting)

and privileges of citizenship'. Thereafter, a two-minute silence was observed in memory of the 'martyrs' in the struggle of freedom.

Then came the moment for which the occasion has always been remembered: the midnight speech by Nehru. In a soft ringing voice, Nehru began speaking words which have since become immortal:

> Long years ago we made a tryst with destiny, and now the time comes when we shall redeem our pledge, not wholly or in full measure, but very substantially. At the stroke of the midnight hour, when the world sleeps, India will awake to life and

Plate 14: Scene from the midnight session. Front row: Amu Swaminathan and G.V. Mavalankar. Back row: Mohanlal Saksena and Pattabhi Sitaramayya (courtesy Photo Division, Ministry of Information and Broadcasting)

Plate 15: Sarvepalli Radhakrishnan addressing the midnight session before the 'Tryst with Destiny' speech (courtesy Photo Division, Ministry of Information and Broadcasting)

Plate 16: Rajendra Prasad presiding over the proceedings of the midnight session (courtesy Photo Division, Ministry of Information and Broadcasting)

Plate 17: Oath of allegiance being taken in the Constituent Assembly. Front row: Sardar Baldev Singh (left) and Jawaharlal Nehru (right) (courtesy Photo Division, Ministry of Information and Broadcasting)

> freedom. A moment which comes but rarely in history, when we step out from the old to the new, when an age ends, and when the soul of a nation, long suppressed, finds utterance. It is fitting that at this solemn moment we take the pledge of dedication to India and her people and to the still larger cause of humanity.[117]

Nehru went on to speak of how the coming of freedom was 'but a step, an opening of opportunity, to but greater triumphs and achievements that await us'. He then posed the question: 'Are we brave enough and wise enough to grasp this opportunity and accept the challenge of the future?' He made a brief but pointed reference to the country's Partition: 'Before the birth of

Plate 18: Jawaharlal Nehru delivering his historic 'Tryst with Destiny' speech (courtesy Photo Division, Ministry of Information and Broadcasting)

freedom we have endured all the pains of labour and our hearts are heavy with the memory of this sorrow. Some of these pains continue even now'. 'Nevertheless, the past is over', he continued, 'and it is the future that beckons to us now'. The future was one of 'incessant striving' to be able to 'fulfil our pledges' in order to bring about 'the ending of poverty and ignorance and disease and inequality of opportunity . . . to wipe every tear from every eye'. He appealed to the 'people of India' to 'join us with faith and confidence in this great adventure' to 'build the noble mansion of free India where all her children may dwell'.

Writers and historians have marvelled at the eloquence with which Nehru was able to capture the feelings and sentiments of millions. His 'Tryst with Destiny' speech has been regarded as a triumph in oratory, an inspired performance which achieved a unique fusion of 'man, mood and moment'.

Nehru then moved a formal resolution, urging that all Assembly members take a pledge of dedication when the midnight hour approached. Chaudhari Khaliquzzaman, a prominent Muslim League leader from UP, rose to support the resolution. He and his party colleagues from the Muslim League had absented themselves from the chamber during the singing of 'Vande Mataram' on grounds that it offended Muslim religious sentiment but had since rejoined the proceedings.[118] In supporting the resolution Khaliquzzaman spoke of the need to be vigilant, as having achieved success in the struggle for freedom, the country was about to embark on 'a new struggle' which is 'not to be fought against any outsider but is to be settled among our own selves'. There lay ahead the challenge of 'framing a Constitution, which would be acceptable not only to the minorities but also to all the people of the country. . . . This is the greatest task'.[119] When he resumed his seat, there was loud cheering. 'Jawaharlal Nehru came to me direct and embraced me heartily for the sentiments I had expressed', recalled Khaliquzzaman.[120]

To second the motion Nehru had chosen Sarvapalli Radhakrishnan, a noted philosopher and educationalist, with the 'the specific directive that, once he was called upon to take the floor, he should not stop till the stroke of midnight so that the assembly could then proceed to take the pledge'.[121] Radhakrishnan took the Assembly through the countdown to midnight for the historic pledge to be taken. His speech was 'an oratorical timebound relay race'. His words echoed the sentiments which Nehru had expressed so lucidly:

> History and legend will grow round this day. It marks a milestone in the march of our democracy. A significant date it is in the drama of the Indian people who are trying to rebuild and transform themselves. Through a long night of waiting, a night full of fateful portents and silent prayers for the dawn of freedom, of haunting specters of hunger and death, our sentinels kept watch, the lights were burning bright till at last the dawn is breaking and we greet it with the utmost enthusiasm. When we are passing from a state of serfdom, a state of slavery and subjection to one of freedom and liberation, it is an occasion for rejoicing.

As Radhakrishnan ended his speech precisely at the twelfth chime of the clock, a conch shell was raucously sounded through the chamber. Nehru rose to administer an oath to members of the Assembly who pledged themselves to the service of the people. Thereafter, the 'national flag' was presented 'on behalf of the women of India' by Hansa Mehta, a prominent women's activist, who expressed the hope: 'May this flag be the symbol of that great India and may it ever fly high. . . . May it bring happiness to those who live under its protecting care'. The singing of 'national songs' followed. The first was Iqbal's famous 'Tarana-e-Hind', whose first few lines, 'Sare Jahan Se Accha Hindustan Hamara', were sung lustily by all. The ceremony ended with the singing of 'Jana Gana Mana', the chosen national anthem.

Outside the Assembly chamber, people were ecstatic. Sham Lal, the veteran journalist, recalled: 'August 1947 was an exciting time; a kind of euphoria had come upon all of us. Delhi was lit up, and we stood around in the streets, waiting for the appointed hour to come. . . . There was a sense of achievement in the air.'[122] Mani Shankar Aiyar, a former diplomat and parliamentarian, was six when his mother took him to watch the midnight ceremonies. Although his memories of that historic night are faint, he was intensely proud 'to have been there at the creation'.[123] Khushwant Singh, the well-known writer, who was also present outside Parliament House, remembered the 'tremendous sense of euphoria and great hope for the future'.[124] Kapila Vatsyayan, an art historian, recalled 'running from Connaught Place that midnight to Central Hall to cheer that great speech' which was 'a great moment of political consciousness of political freedom'.[125] Mulk Raj Anand, the well-known Indian writer, remembers 'the glow of pride' as 'the Tricolour went up'.[126] People listened with rapt attention to the speeches which were being broadcast to those gathered outside. D.F. Karaka, a journalist, recalled: 'Delhi's thousands rejoiced. The town was gay with orange, white and green. Bullocks' and horses' legs were painted in the new national colours and silk merchants sold tri-coloured saris. Triumphant light blazed everywhere, even in the bhangi (untouchable) quarter. Candles and lamps flickered brightly in houses that had never seen an artificial light'. A.K. Damodaran, former diplomat, recalled that 'it was a lovely time to walk in Delhi'.[127] There were countless people who had tuned in to All India Radio to hear a live relay of the proceedings in the baritone voice of Melville de Mellow.

The next morning, on 15 August, the focus shifted to Viceroy's House where Mountbatten, resplendent in official dress, and his wife Edwina, in a shimmering silver gown, entered the Durbar Hall to a fanfare of trumpets. He was sworn in as the new Governor General by the Chief Justice of the Supreme Court. He then administered to Nehru the oath of office as prime minister and thirteen others were sworn in as members of the new Cabinet.

At 9.40 a.m., Mountbatten left in the state coach at the head of a procession for the Constituent Assembly. There he inspected a guard of honour and was received by Prasad. The proceedings began with the reading of messages of greetings from foreign countries. Mountbatten addressed the Assembly in his capacity as the new Governor General. He acknowledged that

Plate 19: Swearing-in ceremony in the Durbar Hall of the Viceroy's Palace on the morning of 15 August 1947. Seen to the left are Nehru and Rajendra Prasad, and to the right are Edwina Mountbatten, Maulana Azad, Sardar Baldev Singh and Syama Prasad Mookerjee (courtesy Photo Division, Ministry of Information and Broadcasting)

the 'advent of freedom is tempered in your hearts by the sadness that it could not come to a united India; and that the pain of division has shorn today's events of some of its joy'.

Prasad then spoke and briefly dwelt upon sentiments of sadness which were being widely felt over Partition. He went on to outline his vision of a new India in which 'poverty and squalor and ignorance and ill-health . . . the distinction between high and low, between rich and poor, will have disappeared', and urged all countrymen to dedicate themselves to the challenge of nation-

Plate 20: Nehru and the Mountbattens at Central Vista on 15 August 1947 (courtesy Nehru Memorial Museum & Library)

building. Thereafter, he invited Mountbatten to give the signal for the hoisting of the 'Tricolour'. A salute of thirty-one guns was fired and the national flag was unfurled over the Council House.

According to reports, flag-hoisting ceremonies took place at more than 300 places all over the city. Many prominent leaders such as J.B. Kripalani, Shankar Rao Deo, G.V. Mavalankar, N.V. Gadgil, S. Radhakrishnan, Ammu Swaminathan, Syed Hussain and Maulana Azad were the guests at several of these. The Congress cadres were particularly enthusiastic. A 2,000-strong corps of Congress Seva Dal volunteers held a rally at Kotla Feroz Shah which was inspected by Sucheta Kripalani. Students and youth sympathetic to the Indian National Army held a flag-hoisting ceremony at Asaf Ali Park in Daryaganj and took out a flag march through

Chandni Chowk. The Delhi Bar Association unfurled the national flag over the district court premises; all kinds of voluntary bodies held their own celebrations. Religious organizations like the Santan Dharma Sabha and the Arya Samaj held special *pujas* and *havans* at several places.

The Christian community, too, showed much enthusiasm. All churches affiliated to the Church of North India and the Delhi Diocese organized special services, the largest being held at the Cathedral Church of the Redemption. A multi-denominational service was held at St. James' Church near Kashmiri Gate. Outside the municipal limits reports were received of enthusiastic participation. From the surrounding countryside people poured into the capital on bullock carts, horse carriages and trucks. Those who stayed on organized functions in their own villages; at Mehrauli, for instance, Gopi Nath 'Aman' presided over the flag ceremony and at Badarpur, Dr Sukh Dev, saluted the 'Tricolour'.

For those who had congregated in the tree-lined streets of Delhi, the highlight of that day was an evening parade organized as an outdoor event to enable the citizens to have a sense of participation. Mountbatten left the Viceroy's House at 6 p.m. in a state carriage, descending an undulating 'King's Way' towards Princess Park near the Memorial Arch. He was received by Nehru and the chief of the army staff. Troops drawn from the three armed services formed a hollow square around the saluting base. A ceremonial Guard of Honour was presented, with military bands

Plate 21: Crowd scenes outside Constituent Assembly in the morning of 15 August 1947 (courtesy Photo Division, Ministry of Information and Broadcasting)

in attendance. Mountbatten inspected the troops, took his salute and returned to the flagstaff where he unfurled the 'Tricolour'. A thirty-one gun salvo was fired. Troops marched past the national flag and a fly-past by fighter planes which dipped in salute followed. A sea of humanity watched the event and, according to eyewitness accounts, a million people had turned up that evening. As the national flag was unfurled, a rainbow flashed across the sky which many interpreted as an auspicious omen. As soon as the parade ended the principal buildings in the vicinity were illuminated. A fireworks display followed towards the western end of King's Way near the Secretariat complex. Many of the prominent city landmarks such as the Memorial Arch,

Plate 22: A photograph of crowd scenes at the inter-services rally at India Gate on the evening of 15 August 1947. Notice the two flags atop India Gate and the canopy to the right, with the statue of King George V, removed in 1968 and replaced in September 2022 by that of Subhas Chandra Bose (courtesy Photo Division, Ministry of Information and Broadcasting)

Plate 23: Women and children at India Gate on the evening of 15 August 1947. In the backdrop is Hyderabad House (courtesy Photo Division, Ministry of Information and Broadcasting)

the Fountain in the old city and the Qutub Minar were illuminated.

While people in the streets lit up their homes, at places of work, public areas, markets and shops an atmosphere of festivity was visible. Mountbatten hosted a dinner reception that evening in Government House. At the banquet, Nehru proposed a toast to the king and Mountbatten reciprocated with a toast to the Dominion of India. After the dinner, Hamid, then on the staff of General Auchinleck, encountered Nawab Ismail Khan, a prominent Muslim League leader from

Plate 24: The Mountbattens, Pamela, Louis and Edwina, watching a juggler's trick in the midst of celebrations at Roshanara Gardens in north Delhi on 15 August 1947 (courtesy Photo Division, Ministry of Information and Broadcasting)

Plate 25: Children getting sweets in Delhi (courtesy Photo Division, Ministry of Information and Broadcasting)

UP, the 'heartland' of the Pakistan campaign. He later recalled:

I was walking through the Moghul Gardens when I noticed a man sitting on a stone bench, with his head bent, smoking a cigarette. To my surprise I found it was Nawab Ismail Khan in deep meditation. I asked him when he was leaving for Pakistan. Very quickly he said that he would stay in India and look after the people who stood by him and voted for him. He felt that such people needed him more now than ever before. He could not let them down. He maintained that some Muslim leaders must stay behind for there were still too many Muslims in India who were not able to dream of going to Pakistan. The simplicity of his statement left me dumbfounded and I admired him all the more.[128]

The next day, on 16 August, the focus shifted to the Red Fort where Nehru addressed a large crowd.

An estimated crowd of one million had gathered to see him raise the 'national flag' over the ramparts of the seventeenth-century Mughal citadel. 'We have gathered here', he began, 'on a historic occasion at this ancient fort to win back what was ours. This flag does not symbolise the triumph of individuals or the Congress but the triumph of the whole country'. According to the historian Jim Masselos, this was a highly symbolic act: 'In one swoop he established a new spatial order, a symbolic taking over of space that had been controlled by the former rulers.'[129] In his speech Nehru declared that:

The first charge of the Government will be to establish and maintain peace and tranquillity in the land and to ruthlessly suppress communal strife. . . . It is wrong to suggest that in this country there would be the rule of a particular religion or

Plate 26: Scene at the Red Fort on the morning of 16 August 1947 (courtesy Photo Division, Ministry of Information and Broadcasting)

Plate 27: Decorations and crowds in Chandni Chowk, Delhi (courtesy Photo Division, Ministry of Information and Broadcasting)

sect. All who owe allegiance to the flag will enjoy equal rights of citizenship, irrespective of caste or creed.[130]

Masselos has perceptively alluded to 'the potency in the symbolism of the Red Fort and in its setting'. He notes that its locale established 'references to the imperial grandeur of the Mughals as well as to the flowering of an imperial state system that was indigenous and therefore national'. This served to highlight 'not merely grandeur by association that the Mughal references underscore' but 'also continuity with a past'. In this sense, 'the new state was legitimised' as 'locating of the

Plate 28: A portrait of Netaji Subhas Chandra Bose with the banner 'Lest we Forget' being carried by INA volunteers to the Red Fort, Delhi, on the morning of 16 August 1947 (courtesy Photo Division, Ministry of Information and Broadcasting)

Plate 29: Crowds at the Red Fort witnessing the flag hoisting by Pandit Jawaharlal Nehru on 16 August 1947 (courtesy Photo Division, Ministry of Information and Broadcasting)

Plate 30: Crowd control arrangements between the intersection of Red Fort and Chandni Chowk on 16 August 1947 (courtesy Photo Division, Ministry of Information and Broadcasting)

Plate 31: Crowds assembling on 16 August 1947 at the Red Fort (courtesy Photo Division, Ministry of Information and Broadcasting)

Plate 32: Edwina Mountbatten, Nehru and others at the Red Fort (courtesy Photo Division, Ministry of Information and Broadcasting)

Plate 33: Nehru before news photographers at the Red Fort (courtesy Photo Division, Ministry of Information and Broadcasting)

main independence day gathering at the Fort asserts an historical legitimacy to the new nation and implies an identity that does not derive from the British interregnum'.

Masselos has also unravelled several other symbolic elements such as the memories of the Revolt of 1857 with which the Fort was associated which, in his view, marked a 'redressing of the balance of justice'. Further, Nehru in his speech recalled Subhas Chandra Bose who had 'sacrificed and suffered' and lamented that though he 'hoisted this flag in foreign countries and when the day came for hoisting it on the Red Fort, he was not there to see his dream fulfilled'. Masselos notes that by remembering Bose, Nehru made an emotional connection to the Indian National Army whose men he had defended in a trial conducted at the Red Fort a few years ago. Above all, the ceremony signified 'the march to freedom' and 'assumptions of power'.[131]

There is evidence, though, that there were different ways in which the symbolism of the events was being interpreted. For instance, many Muslims viewed the ceremony at the Red Fort in a remarkably different way. Ashfaq Alam Khan of Meerut captured some of these concerns when he wrote to the *Dawn* to protest against the use of the Red Fort:

> It is reported that the Union Jack on the Red Fort will be replaced by the Congress flag on Aug. 15. This historic building of red stone and marble stands on the sandy bank of the Jummna in sacred memory of centuries of Muslim rule in India and is held in high esteem by the Muslims all over the country. The Union Jack which was hoisted after bloody hand-to-hand fighting in the streets of Delhi during the Mutiny and

which had flown throughout since then will at last be lowered from this memorable fort, and at that hour it is advisable that the over-zealous Congressmen should refrain from playing with Muslim sentiments, especially in the present atmosphere of mutual suspicion and hatred. The flags of both the dominions should be hoisted in the fort or none at all. The Red Fort like other historic buildings is an Archaeological monument and should be placed under joint control.[132]

Two days later the *Dawn* raised the issue in its editorial. It declared that the plan to raise the flag of the Indian union on 16 August at the Red Fort had 'caused considerable agitation among the Muslims'. It was noted that it 'would have been far more graceful of the Nehru government if they had respected deeply the sentiments and desisted from hoisting their flag on this historical monument in such haste'. It sounded a note of caution and warning when it observed: 'We trust that there will be no petty-minded jubilation by the Hindus under the mistaken impression that by hoisting the flag of their state on the seat of power of ancient Muslim Kings they have somehow stretched a spiteful hand back into the historic past and dimmed the imperishable glory of Muslim rule.'[133]

In fact, the use of the Red Fort as a site for raising the flag was seen by many as controversial, and several Muslim leaders had hoped that such a move would be avoided. For instance, Sham Mohammed Siddique, an honorary magistrate in Delhi, had suggested to the authorities that the 'national flag of Hindustan' should be hoisted on the bandstand at Connaught Place, and that the 'unfurling ceremony should be performed by a prominent Muslim'. Likewise, in the memoirs of Khaliquzzaman, there is lament at the state of 'Delhi of the Mughal emperors in 1947'.[134] Similarly, Begum Shaista Ikramullah recalls that 'for millions of people like myself, Delhi was 'synonymous with Muslim culture'.[135] Perhaps such concerns over use of the city's most prominent indigenous building reflected a deeper sense of unease which the ceremony on 16 August caused to Muslim sentiments.

On the evening of 16 August, the Red Fort witnessed a brilliant display of fireworks. Over half a million people observed a spectacle which included dazzling items like 'Searchlight' and 'Waterfall by Moon Light' which the organizers proudly claimed were 'purely made with Swadeshi stuffs [*sic*] and with Hindustani skill'.[136] While there were many who were ecstatic at such glittery expressions of joy, there was present within the city a significant Muslim population which perhaps took a somewhat different view of what was happening. How did they respond to such extravagant exhibitions of joy? Were they apprehensive about their place in these celebrations, their right of residence, the safety of their families and homes, and their status as citizens of the new nation? To add to their sense of nervousness and foreboding, there were already present in Delhi, on the eve of Independence, an estimated 100,000 refugees, who had taken asylum in the capital to escape violence. According to reports, thousands were pouring in every day—Hindus and Sikhs from different riot-affected areas in the NWFP and West Punjab as well as Muslims from districts of East Punjab and the princely states of

Alwar and Bharatpur.[137] The city's rationing authorities had been inundated by requests for ration cards while civic authorities feared the outbreak of a public health crisis.[138] There refugees provided a stark counterpoint to the burst of fireworks and collective expressions of joy which dominated the celebrations in the capital.

Beyond Capitals

We could perhaps look beyond the capital cities to see how other places were experiencing the events of 14–15 August. Bombay was one city where celebrations were particularly impressive and remarkable scenes of popular enthusiasm were witnessed. The city had, after all, been a stronghold of Congress activity. Moreover, as a metropolis with a population drawn from several communities, regions and classes, it had a composite public culture, invigorated by the presence of a large middle class.

In Bombay, preparations had been made for the official ceremonies by Morarji Desai, the home minister, and S.K. Patil, president of the Bombay Pradesh Congress Committee. At a press conference Desai had outlined the programme which mostly conformed to the format prescribed by New Delhi. He declared that 'Vande Mataram' would not be sung at public functions as it had been decided not to 'offend the susceptibilities of any people'. At the precise midnight hour, sirens from ships and factories were to alert the people and a military parade was to take place on 15 August. Likewise, the unofficial programme drawn by Patil on behalf of the Bombay Congress had included the hoisting of the national flag on Congress House and other public buildings at five minutes past midnight, garlanding of statues of national 'heroes', observance of a two-minute silence in the memory of national 'martyrs', processions and a meeting in the evening to be held at the Oval Maidan at Churchgate.

As in other places, the atmosphere in Bombay had been marked by anxiety for the city's Muslim residents. On Friday, 5 August, a bomb blast had occurred in Taj Talkies where the film *Arab-ka-Sitara* was showing. The explosion killed five persons and injured over 160. The following evening another crude bomb had exploded near a mosque as the congregation was dispersing after prayers. Finally, on Sunday, a third bomb was lobbed at a mosque in the densely populated area of Chindi Bazar, with several casualties. These incidents heightened the sense of apprehension which the Muslim residents felt as they looked to the coming of 15 August.[139] Nonetheless, several prominent Muslim leaders sought to allay these fears and urged the Muslims to ignore calls of boycotting the celebrations and to participate wholeheartedly in them. The lead was given by Hassanally P. Ibrahim, the president of the Bombay Provincial Muslim League, who joined the official committee formed by the Bombay Government to formally associate the Muslims with the programme of celebrations.[140] Likewise, His Holiness Sardar Saifuddin Saheb, the chief of the Dawoodi Bohra community, which had a strong presence in city, issued instructions to his followers to participate in the celebrations.

On the night of 14 August, an impressive ceremony was organized from 9 p.m. onwards at the Congress House on V.J. Patel Road. The function started with the singing of 'Vande Mataram'. At exactly midnight sirens from factories and ships docked in the harbour signalled the arrival of the 'appointed hour' and crackers and gongs 'announced the arrival of freedom'. Patil, the chief organizer of the function, had wanted a religious ceremony to mark the beginning of the new era and had searched for 'qualified brahmans' suitable for the occasion who would chant mantras from the Vedas appropriate for the occasion. However, he was persuaded to alter his plan and instead to have a multi-faith function in which hymns from the Quran, the Bible, the Zenda Avesta and the Vedas were included. The rituals of the secular state were being invented!

Karaka, a noted city journalist, recalls that 'there was something different' that evening as 'it was difficult not to be conscious of the moment towards which we were moving'. On his way back from work he saw that 'floral arches spanned the main roads and festoons were strung across streets and lanes. Colourful buntings and streamers waved everywhere'. He could notice crowded streets as people headed home. 'Workmen and common people. . . . That evening they would bathe and anoint themselves as for a holy fiesta. Caste and out-caste, capitalist and labourer, city man and peasant all had the same idea'. That evening Karaka found himself at a banquet hosted by the mayor of Bombay at the Taj Mahal Hotel. Close to midnight the place was darkened and, as the clock sounded twelve, the lights came on and the 'Tricolour' was illuminated. Outside, people thronged the streets: 'That wide open space between the Taj Mahal Hotel and the Gateway of India was one solid block. The bright lights of the illuminations fell on them. From the harbour the ships were throwing searchlights on the land. . . . What a night it was! With the crowds refusing to go home.'[141]

The crowd scenes were equally memorable the next day. Khwaja Ahmad Abbas, a journalist and great grandson of the Muslim poet and thinker Altaaf Hussain Hali, woke up worried whether it would rain on that historic day. The newspapers carried in headlines reports about Nehru's midnight speech. Abbas recalls: 'I did not know then that as he was uttering these stirring words he carried in his sherwani pocket the telegrams from Punjab, UP, Bihar and Bengal about the atrocities that continued to be committed against Hindus and Sikhs, and against Muslims.'[142] He joined the main procession and discovered that 'All [of] Bombay was at Gowalia Tank.' About a million people were present in the 3 mi. procession. Abbas joined a group of writers and artistes; everyone was singing and dancing. Patil recalls that 'the celebrations continued for four days without let or hindrance. There were crowds everywhere in the city streets. Bombay, as only Bombay can, outdid all other cities'.[143]

Masselos notes that in Bombay 'those who partici pated in the rites of passage were wildly enthusiastic'. His work brings out the strong communitarian spirit in the celebrations at Bombay, expressed in the holding of special caste dinners and family feasts, large scale distribution of sweets to 'the unprivileged and the down and out, the harijans and the beggars of the city' which was made possible by the donations of wealthy businessmen. This spirit was reflected in the way crowds roamed the city.

> Obviously they were celebrating, and celebrating by being together, a feature common to past religious festivals in the city, but they were also looking at the city in a different way, moving all around it as their own, whereas the space they took over in religious festivals was often limited and demarcated to specific localities. This was not the case in August 1947 as the entire city was re-defined subconsciously as the total territorial bounds of the new nation.[144]

Perhaps it may be useful to look at the celebrations in a different setting, to be able to get a sense of the diverse perceptions of 14–15 August across the subcontinent. The example of Dhaka, over a thousand miles away from Bombay, enables us to do so. In the city of Dhaka, where the East Pakistan Government was trying to establish its base, a sense of unease prevailed. An atmosphere of uncertainty seemed to have enveloped the 'minority' communities there. Although there had been no confirmed reports, the air was rent with rumours of a 'considerable flight of capital', of properties being sold and of an impending 'mass exodus'. One especially worrisome rumour doing its rounds was that, with the establishment of Pakistan on 14 August, all Hindu properties would automatically pass into the hands of Muslims.[145] Anxieties mounted even further when news broke that all Hindu government employees had elected to serve the Indian Union and would, thus, soon be leaving. As they already had an assurance from the premier of West Bengal that they would be accommodated in the new province, the minorities feared that the city police force would be devoid of a single Hindu police officer.

The widespread sense of anxiety brought together influential Hindu public figures in Dhaka to hold a convention at the Narayanganj Bar Academy to demand protection of the 'minorities' and that steps be taken to 'keep up the morale of the people'. They demanded from the Indian authorities guarantees of help 'including the conferment on the minority of East Bengal the right of citizenship in all areas within the Indian Union'.[146] Another meeting later in the week was held at the Rupmahal cinema hall under the auspices of the Dhaka Congress Committee. Taking note of the panicky situation, Congressmen decided to tour rural areas to allay fears, to form 'strong volunteer corps' and called upon all non-Muslim members of the Pakistan Constituent Assembly and the East Bengal Legislative Assembly to reside in their respective constituencies to 'restore confidence'. However, the sense of panic persisted. By early August, monies deposited in banks and commercial houses were being withdrawn in large amounts.

Politicians in East Bengal attempted to allay the panic. On 30 July a large public meeting had been jointly organized at Mymensingh by the Congress and the Muslim League. Appeals had been made to Hindus to stay, as well as to the Muslims not to permit the 'minorities' to leave because of 'foolish acts of aggression' but to seek their 'co-operation in the development of the state of East Pakistan with its poor resources'. Those present included S.M. Ghosh, president of the Bengal Congress and Moulvi Sharifuddin Ahmed, chairman of the district board. The latter had assured that the new state would be governed on principles of justice and equity and that Hindus and Muslims would have their separate personal laws.[147] Likewise, the Hindu Mahasabha also organized a convention at the Shyama Prasad Mukherjee University Hall. Its leader S.P. Mukherjee had demanded that Pakistani authorities make constitutional provisions to safeguard the 'political, religious and economic rights' of the 'minorities'. He had wanted the Government of East Bengal to explicitly declare that it had no intention to confiscate capital or properties belonging to non-Muslims. Mukherjee had advised only those Hindus to leave their homes where they were 'hopelessly small in number and to migrate to other places and form pockets'. Hindu landowners were to give land for setting up such pockets, women were to be removed from places where 'their honour might be in danger' and students were asked to give up their studies for a month to go to villages and 'help in maintaining the morale of the rural people'.[148] On 2 August, the Dhaka Central Peace Committee had met to take stock of the situation. It reiterated Jinnah and other League leaders' assurances to the minorities that there was no cause for panic.[149]

Such had been the mood in Dhaka when plans for the Independence Day celebrations were being worked out. A twelve-member committee had been appointed by the Bengal Muslim League to organize the inaugural celebrations of Pakistan and to welcome the East Bengal

Government to the city. Khwaja Habibullah, the ex-Nawab of Dhaka, had been appointed president of the committee.[150] Meanwhile, the Bengal Congress had sent out its own specific instructions on how celebrations were to take place in East Bengal. It had directed for the joint hoisting of the Congress flag and the flag of Pakistan. In other matters the initiative had been left to local leaders. All bans on meetings and processions were to be respected and all conflicting situations avoided. Celebrations were to be voluntary and no compulsion was to be exercised. It was, it said, 'advisable to cancel the celebration altogether rather than give opportunity for any unhappy incident'.[151] Four prominent Congress leaders, including J.C. Gupta, a member of the Bengal Legislative Assembly, had been deputed to help the local Congress at Dhaka with regard to the celebrations.[152] Further clarifications followed by Kalipada Mukherjee, Secretary of the Bengal Provincial Congress Committee, who made it clear that the minorities 'as loyal citizens of the State in all private houses on any day of State celebration, as on the fifteenth they should give due recognition to the State Flag'.[153]

On 15 August 'Pakistan Independence Day' was marked in Dhaka with the hoisting of the flag by Khwaja Habibullah, formerly Nawab of Dhaka, at the historic Lalbag Fort, an old Mughal palace. Pakistani flags were hoisted on government buildings, many of which were decorated. In a number of Hindu localities, the Congress flag flew alongside the new Pakistan flag. Decorated arches named after prominent martyrs were erected at many places. The official ceremonies went off smoothly and no untoward incidents were reported, except one instance of pulling down of a Congress flag.[154]

On the same day the swearing in of the new government took place at Curzon Hall. Justice Akram, Chief Justice of the East Bengal High Court, administered the oath of office to Sir Fredrick C. Bourne, the new governor. Also sworn in were the new premier, Khwaja Nazimuddin, and two of his ministers, Nurul Amin and Hamidul Huq Chowdhury. The speeches made at the ceremony alluded to the great responsibilities that lay ahead. Sir Fredrick spoke of East Bengal as a 'young province' in which 'many difficult, many urgent problems will present themselves'; however, he continued, 'you have the advantages of youth, enthusiasm, energy and high ideals'. Nazimuddin admitted that the magnitude of the tasks which awaited the new government were enormous. He assured the 'minorities' of 'honorable and generous' treatment. The swearing-in ceremony concluded with recitations from the Holy Quran and the unfurling of the Pakistan flag by the governor.[155]

On 16 August there was a public meeting at Victoria Park where Khwaja Nazimuddin unfurled the Pakistan flag. He spoke of communal violence as a 'thing of the past' now that freedom had arrived. The common rejoicing by members of different communities for Independence had filled his heart with 'great hope' and convinced him that confidence was being restored. He further assured the minorities of a 'fair and generous deal'. So confident was he that he was prepared to withdraw all cases and collective fines and to release those convicted in communal affrays, if representatives of Hindus and Muslims jointly put forth the demand. However, he warned that 'he had no Aladdin's lamp or a magic wand to transform the country'. Nazimuddin's speech was followed by officials and leaders of opposition parties. B. Das Gupta, Chairman of Dhaka Municipality, assured the cooperation of the minorities and warned that freedom could not be retained if there was any oppression of the minority community. Leela Roy, leader of the Forward Bloc, assured the prime minister of the cooperation of her party; D.N. Barori, ex-minister, extended support on behalf of the Scheduled Castes' Federation, and Nepal Nag spoke for the Communists.

In a broadcast which he made later in the day from the Dhaka Station of the Pakistan Broadcasting Service, Nazimuddin expressed similar sentiments and asked all Muslims to work in unison and invoke the blessings of God for the tasks that lay ahead.[156] A procession was taken through the main streets. Starting from Chowk, it passed through Moghultully, Mitford Road, Islampur Road and Johnson Road, and many participants raised slogans such as '*Azad Pakistan Zindabad*', '*Quaid-i-Azam Zindabad*' and '*Hindus-Muslims are brothers*'. The procession ended at Victoria Park.[157]

From all accounts it appears that the ceremonies in Dhaka, which had been a backwater in the Muslim League campaign to establish Pakistan, had been confined largely to the staging of state rituals marking the establishment of Pakistan and the assumption of power by a new government. The element of popular participation, so strikingly evident in other places, for instance Bombay, was noticeably missing. In retrospect, one could see that events in Dhaka did not go beyond signalling the city's affirmation of Pakistan and its place as a part of that territory.

In looking for divergent responses to the celebrations, it is striking that at many places there was a fusion of official ceremonies and popular elements which produced certain remarkable scenes. One place where a strong popular element coalesced extraordinarily well with official rituals was in Banaras, one of the holiest cities in India. According to reports, 'flag-bedecked Banaras went riotous with colour and gaiety as India shook off the shackles of slavery at midnight'. The countdown to midnight was greeted with the blowing of conch shells and the incessant ringing of temple bells in the hundreds of temples situated in the holy city. On the morning of 15 August official ceremonies commenced at the Police Lines where Nisar Ahmad Sherwani, a cabinet minister in UP, inspected the Guard of Honour. Later, at another large gathering he hoisted the 'Tricolour' over the district court in the presence of district officials. The City Congress organized its own celebrations at the Town Hall where men from the Special Armed Constabulary presented a Guard of Honour to the national flag. Away from the city, the students of Banaras Hindu University, which had been a storm centre in the 'Quit India' movement of 1942, held their own ceremony where the prominent Congress leader Sampurnanand unfurled the flag at the Amphitheatre.

In the afternoon the focus shifted to the unique

Bharat Mata Temple where a highly symbolic ceremony marked the coming of Independence. The temple, dedicated to 'Mother India', is extraordinary in that its inner sanctum contains no deity of the Hindu pantheon but rather a large iconic representation of *Bharat Mata* depicting the 'bounties of nature bestowed upon the land'.[158] A large relief map shows the key physical features of 'Mother India', rimmed by the Himalayas and watered by the Ganges and 'other holy rivers of heaven'. The 'sacred geography' of *Bharat Mata* is demarcated by the *dhams* (abodes of gods), located in the four directions, a visit to which is known as *Mahaparikrama* (the great pilgrimage). Visitors to the temple first circumambulate the relief map and then climb to the second-floor balcony for its *darshan*.[159]

In a ceremony marked by enthusiasm, N.A. Sherwani, a Muslim Congressman, unfurled the flag over the Bharat Mata Temple in the presence of a huge crowd. In the evening the focus shifted to Dashashwamedh Ghat, the most popular of the bathing ghats along the Ganges where, according to legend, Brahma the Creator, had performed *ashwamedh yagna* (Vedic ritual sacrifice of horses), marking the earliest consecration according to Hindu legends. From this spot, one of the holiest in Hinduism, where a dip in the Ganges destroys the sins of a lifetime for a believer, started a huge torchlight procession. This procession, 'the biggest in living memory' marched through Chowk and the main thoroughfares and terminated at Town Hall, where the local Congress leaders held a public meeting around the Martyrs' Memorial.[160]

A similar pattern was evident in Agra, another city in UP. Here, the highlight was the hoisting of the 'Tricolour' by the military commandant of Agra on the Mughal Fort. A flag-raising ceremony was also held at the Ram Lila grounds where more than 300,000 people were present. At the Police Lines, Jagan Prasad Rawat, a parliamentary secretary in the UP cabinet, inspected a parade and unfurled the flag. At the municipal office, the programme included recitations from the Vedas and the *Bhagwat Gita*. A police parade marched through the city at the head of a 2 mi. long procession led by local Congress leaders which terminated at the Ram Lila grounds in a public meeting addressed by Seth Achal Singh, president of the city Congress.[161]

'Mahatma's Miracle'

Several hundreds of miles away in eastern India, Calcutta was in a different mood on the eve of Independence. It had suddenly become the focus of attention as Mahatma Gandhi had arrived in the city 'to rescue it from the danger of communal violence'. When Gandhi had decided to absent himself from the state rituals being staged in New Delhi, he had hoped to be in Noakhali in East Bengal, a riot-torn area where he had for several months concentrated his energies to bring about 'Hindu-Muslim unity'. However, as a result of unexpected circumstances, he now found himself in Calcutta. For almost a year since the 'Direct Action' day killings of 16 August 1946, Calcutta had been living through a nightmare. For months the city had been subjected to more than its fair share of communal animosity, with violence erupting frequently in the charged atmosphere. The bitterness and hostility were, to a large extent, compounded by the uncertainty about the future of the city, as rival claims had been made over it before the Boundary Commission. In the context of Bengal, Calcutta had become the epicentre of the boundary disputes. Although the population of the city had a clear Hindu majority, the Muslim League had made an impassioned plea to the Boundary Commission to have Calcutta included in Pakistan.[162] As Independence drew near, the signs were ominous, Calcutta was on the verge of a civil war and any spark of trouble on Independence Day could well trigger it off.

Faced with such circumstances, the leaders of the provisionally divided West and East Bengal knew the urgency of the tasks that lay ahead in the run up to Independence. It was not so much about planning and organizing the celebratory events; rather the realization that the utmost had to be done by Muslim League and Congress leaders to prevent the occasion from slipping into an ostensible demonstration of communal victory by one group over the other, which became the priority. In their concern of not wanting the Independence Day celebrations to become an occasion and excuse for communal clashes, Muslim League and Congress organizations in Bengal had issued injunctions to their followers, reminding them to be sensitive to the feelings of 'minorities' during the celebrations. The Bengal Congress circulated instructions to its district committees, particularly in north and east Bengal and in Sylhet district, which were expected to go to Pakistan, that they should raise the Congress flag, and the Pakistan state flag alongside it.[163] While no one was to be forced to take part in the celebrations, the Bengal Congress Committee urged its supporters to make special efforts to maintain 'an atmosphere of communal amity'.[164] Likewise, the Bengal Provincial Muslim League issued its own directions on how Independence Day was to be observed in East Bengal. The Pakistan national flag was to be raised on all houses and buildings. A special prayer was to be offered to invoke the blessings of Allah for the new state of Pakistan, and processions were to be planned at various places. Jinnah, however, ordained that, while Muslims need not sing 'Vande Mataram', they should 'continue enthusiastic participation in the celebrations'.[165]

Notwithstanding the political parties expecting to achieve a degree of cordiality with each other, the situation on the ground remained as tense as ever. Muhammad Usman, secretary of the Calcutta Muslim League, complained that, despite hopes that the coming of Independence would bring about a return to peace and normality, the city was still in a disturbed state, with the Muslim 'minority' bearing the brunt of 'Hindu hatred'. In a press statement he pointed out that 'life [in] the city [was] far from satisfactory' and 'disturbances [were] continuing unabated, with minorities . . . forced to leave their hearths and homes'.[166] At a meeting on 10 August, Maulana Muhammed Yahya, president of the Calcutta Muslim League, claimed that hundreds of *bustees* in Calcutta and Howrah had been 'destroyed by bombs, firearms and arson' and that several hundreds of Muslims had been made homeless.[167] Women and children had been the targets of attacks by Hindu mobs, and several of their places of worship had been defiled and demolished.[168]

Propaganda had begun to gather ground that the new West Bengal administration was bent on an anti-Muslim policy. The glaring absence of Muslim officers from the administrative structure, including the Calcutta police force, gave rise to the charge that a Hindu *raj* was being created in West Bengal. This was seen as a manifestation of the feeling among Congress leaders that they had established a great communal victory over the 'minorities' of Calcutta, who must be treated as their vanquished enemy.[169] The Muslim minority in Calcutta had lost faith in the ability, indeed the willingness, of the West Bengal administration to provide protection and security to the community. For them, the prospects of survival in Calcutta after Independence appeared grim. Given the situation, the Calcutta Muslim League threatened that, if such a state of affairs persisted and the safety of Muslim life and property remained threatened, it would issue a call to the Muslims of Calcutta not to join in the celebrations of Independence, but instead to mark the day by silence, as a black day of mourning.[170] They promised, however, that the Muslims would not oppose nor obstruct the official celebrations, and there would be no violence or demonstration on their part; the protest would be carried out in a peaceful and dignified manner.[171]

Such was the atmosphere of communal rancour and bitterness in Calcutta that greeted Gandhi when he arrived in the city on 9 August on his way to Noakhali.

His coming was regarded by several Muslim leaders as a godsend. Fearing that they would be at the mercy of the majority come Independence Day, they begged Gandhi to stay on to use his personal presence and moral influence 'to pour a pot of water on the raging fire' that was consuming the city.[172]

Shaheed Suhrawardy, leader of the Bengal Muslim League and the man whom many Hindus blamed for precipitating the massacres of 'Direct Action' day in 1946, flew from Karachi, upon hearing of Gandhi's visit, to be able to persuade the Mahatma to stay on until peace could be restored in the city. Gandhi was at first reluctant, claiming that there were more pressing needs in Noakhali. However, the anxieties of Muslims and the tense situation convinced him that he was needed there, and he agreed to stay for a few days. At the same time, he imposed two conditions. First, he wanted the Muslims in Calcutta to assure him that they would do all they could to maintain peace in Noakhali. He elicited from their leaders a promise that they would send telegrams to their co-religionists in Noakhali to stop them from taking any action against the Hindus there.[173] This was agreed to, with the added promise that personal emissaries would also be sent to Noakhali to keep the peace at the first signs of trouble.[174] Gandhi further insisted that Suhrawardy stay by his side throughout his stopover in Calcutta to work for Hindu–Muslim unity and to show that both the Congress and the Muslim League were working together towards peace. When both these conditions were met, Gandhi took up residence at Hydari Manzil at 151 Beliaghata Road in a predominantly Hindu district. Not far from his house was Miabagan, a Muslim slum, which had recently been raided by young Hindus armed with homemade grenades and Sten guns borrowed from former soldiers.[175]

When he heard the woes of Calcutta and tales of the 'recital of man's barbarism' it made his 'head hang in shame'. He was told that although the population of Calcutta was more than 23 per cent Muslim, there were parts of the city which were inaccessible to the Hindus; that the Hindus had begun to feel that they were free to retaliate now that Muslim policemen and officers had almost withdrawn and been replaced by Hindus; and that the 'wretched spirit of communalism' had entered even the police force.[176]

Gandhi's worst fears seemed to be coming true. He had been, from the outset, as is well known, opposed to the vivisection of the country. He had vehemently challenged Jinnah's 'two-nation' theory, arguing that India was not a nation but a civilization. He had always maintained that the idea that the Muslims and Hindus constituted separate 'nations' and should have their own states was 'preposterous and impractical'.[177] He pointed out that, even if the subcontinent were to be divided on the basis of religious nationalism, the new state of Pakistan would have to include a large number of Hindus, just as millions of Muslims would be left in India. The solution lay not in division but in finding a way of accommodating the minorities. Despite Gandhi's tremendous moral influence at the time, there was little he could do to overcome a communal estrangement that had become so deep that it ensured that 'all well-meaning constitutional schemes collapsed without a fair trial'.[178] In the end, the only acceptable alternative was the dreaded one of Partition. When the Congress Working Committee had decided to accept the 3 June Plan, accepting the 'inevitability' of the country's Partition, Gandhi had declared that he would not stand in the way of a decision that had been collectively made, although he disagreed with it. He could see that 'impatience with independence' had driven the Congress to accept the 'evil of Partition'.[179] He had on that occasion cautioned: 'Should the evil I apprehend overtake India and her independence be imperiled, let posterity know what agony this old man went through thinking of it. Let not the coming generations curse Gandhi for being a party to India's vivisection.'[180]

Gandhi had resisted Partition because the idea, according to him, rested on the inherently evil principle of religious nationalism, 'denying a thousand years of Indian history', with its traditions of plurality, diversity and tolerance. More importantly, he feared that Partition would only generate more anger and bitterness between Muslims and non-Muslims which would lead to violence and bloodshed.[181] However, as the bulk of the Congress leadership accepted Partition, Gandhi had acquiesced in it.

Having accepted the decision, Gandhi interpreted it in a different way. He had taken it upon himself to persuade the people not to look upon the act of Partition and the creation of Pakistan with revenge and anger. He portrayed it as the splitting up of a Hindu joint family. As family members could not live together, they were free to set up separate households to avoid constant quarrels. But separation did not mean that these family members should hate and kill each other, and deny their common history.[182] Repeatedly, at prayer meetings over the months, Gandhi had exhorted his listeners not to consider India and Pakistan as two separate countries; the division of land, which was a physical and political act, should not lead to a division of hearts.[183] As long as men's hearts remained true, he urged, they could behave as if there had been no Partition of the country.[184] He regarded, in particular, the division of the armed forces as 'an error and a terrible mistake', for it would not lead to mutual peace between the two countries, but was likely to generate mutual fear and mistrust and cause future conflicts.[185] He could accept that India and Pakistan would be two separate states, but to him they would never be two different nations.[186]

Yet Gandhi knew, all along, that he was working against heavy odds.[187] The passions had been aroused to such intensity that, to him, violence and bloodshed seemed imminent. The signs were everywhere: in Lahore, Hindus were evacuating in large numbers; elsewhere in northern India 'the pent-up emotions of hundreds of thousands of people were being expressed in acts of casual violence'.[188] In Calcutta he could see that 'young blood is boiling'.[189] As soon as he had taken residence in Hydari Manzil, he had a taste of the undercurrents of rage. As he entered the place he was met with 'cries of traitor and a shower of bottles and stones'.[190] Angry Hindu youths accused him of coming to Calcutta in defence of Muslims. The angry crowds demanded to know why he had not gone to places where Hindus were the victims? They accused him of being a traitor who was interested only in the Muslims and asked him to leave Beliaghata. Patiently, Gandhi remonstrated with the angry deputations that continuously came crowding around the house. Speaking in well-attended prayer meetings, he asked for tolerance; he argued that, although India was getting Independence soon, she would not become free unless all its communities could live in peace beside each other. Gandhi's presence somewhat allayed the anger amongst the Hindus, but it was clear that many were still resentful. Their anger dissipated, however, when Suhrawardy, during a public speech on the eve of Independence, admitted that he had been responsible for the killings on 'Direct Action' day. The admission, according to Gandhi, was the turning point and had a 'cleansing effect'.[191]

The calming influence that Gandhi exerted by his sheer presence in Calcutta was beginning to have its impact. With Suhrawardy by his side, he seemed to have dissipated the anger of the Hindus as well as allayed the fears of the Muslims. On the eve of Independence day, the mutual hatred and anger which had prevailed in Calcutta for nearly a year seemed to have evaporated. People started venturing onto the streets, evidently encouraged by the surprising absence of violence, and the whole city suddenly took on a holiday-like mood, with plenty of demonstrable amity between the two communities.[192] News soon reached Gandhi that over 5,000 Muslims and a similar number of Hindus were marching in peace through the city.[193]

It was a matter of some pride that Gandhi had managed to bring sanity to the city on the occasion when the dream to which he had dedicated his life—the

Independence of India from colonial rule—was about to be realized. Yet, he confessed that, as India's freedom and her day of deliverance from the 'foreign yoke' drew near, he was filled with a sense of foreboding, and all that he saw was darkness everywhere.[194] He knew that at the hour of Independence, India would be subjected to the supreme test, as that freedom would contain the seeds of future conflict between India and Pakistan.[195] He would not celebrate, but would mark the occasion with a day of fasting, spinning and praying. He invited everyone to embark on a 'twenty four hour fast and prayer' and to spin 'as much as possible'. On the night of 14 August he went to bed as usual, refusing to await the countdown to the midnight ceremonies. 'At the stroke of the midnight hour, when the world sleeps, India will awake to life and freedom': when Nehru uttered these famous words, the 'Father of the Nation' was fast asleep, having deliberately forsaken the glitter of the state rituals being staged with pomp and ceremony in New Delhi.

The next morning, on 15 August, Gandhi's thoughts were filled with sorrow; five years earlier on that very day, Mahadev Desai, his secretary for twenty-five years and the 'tallest' of his disciples, had passed away suddenly while in detention at the Aga Khan Palace. Gandhi had himself lit his funeral pyre.[196] His spirits lifted when he saw that the goodwill and peace achieved on 14 August spilled into Independence Day. Calcutta was wrapped in a friendly atmosphere and ecstatic scenes of togetherness were witnessed in the streets which were jammed with people out to celebrate and chant exuberantly, 'Hindu-Muslim *bhai bhai!*' and 'Long live Hindustan and

Pakistan!'[197] Gandhi's home at Beliaghata saw a stream of visitors throughout the day: Hindus, Muslims, the new Governor C. Rajagopalachari, the new ministry of West Bengal headed by Prafulla Ghosh, students and Communists. Gandhi advised the new government to be humble and forbearing and to 'beware of power'. He asked them not to be 'entrapped by its pomp and pageantry' but to always remember that they were in office 'to serve the poor in India's villages'.[198]

A large congregation awaited him in the evening at his prayer meeting at Rash Bagan Maidan to which he insisted on walking. He congratulated the city on the fraternization which it was witnessing on that day. Muslims and Hindus were, he noted, meeting in 'perfect friendliness'; they all shouted the same slogans and flew the same 'Tricolour'; Hindus were being admitted to mosques and Muslims to Hindu mandirs. Gandhi was reminded of the days of the Khilafat movement: 'If this exhibition was from the heart and was not a momentary impulse, it was better than the Khilafat days', since, he said, both communities had 'drunk the poison cup of disturbances' and the 'nectar of friendliness should, therefore, taste sweeter than before'. Gandhi hoped this heralded the end to disturbances and that Calcutta could, henceforth, be 'entirely free from the communal virus' and offer an example to other parts of the country like the Punjab.[199] The widespread scenes of celebration in the streets and the mood of the day amazed those present in the city. The American Consul in Calcutta who witnessed many of the events pointed out that 'in view of the delicate balance which had existed only a few hours before' the transformation which had come about was 'miraculous' and was 'in no sense an overstatement'.[200] He noted:

> With the advent of independence, communal peace in Calcutta was miraculously restored. Fraternisation on the friendliest basis and on a tremendous scale erased overnight a full year's heritage of murder, death and destruction has completely transformed the city and the outlook of its people…the whole city was in a holiday spirit…. Dominion flags appeared from nowhere to be flown on every building, bus tram and automobile and many demonstrations of amity between the two communities which only a few hours previously had been engaged in cutting each other's throats were witnessed everywhere. . . . Gandhi is widely credited with being the wizard responsible for the magical transformation of Calcutta. Vast public meetings are held in Calcutta and vicinity practically every day, at which, after the conclusion of his prayer meeting, Gandhi gives his views. . . . The attendance at these rallies is tremendous; one is believed to have attracted half a million people.[201]

Mountbatten publicly commended his efforts in a broadcast, waxing lyrical about his miraculous 'one-man boundary force who kept the peace while a 50,000 strong force was swamped by riots'.

Meanwhile, the key event symbolic of the British withdrawal from Calcutta took place with an unusual burst of popular fervour. Its scene was Government House, where a flag-raising ceremony and a ceremonial farewell to the British Governor, Sir Frederic Burrows, had been scheduled on the morning of 15 August. In attendance was 'all the city's great and near great'. Such was the popular enthusiasm that the crowds overtook the place. The American consul recalled that a 'rabble broke out to take over the Government House, infiltrating into every nook and cranny'.[202] Order broke down and the crowds simply took over the palatial building, one of the grandest examples of colonial architecture in the subcontinent, and they allegedly helped themselves to 'souvenirs'. 'Among the various stories is one to the effect that Lady Burrows, emerging from the bathroom found three unwashed Indians peacefully reposing in her bed.'[203]

Here was one example of what Masselos calls the 'breaking down [of] the boundaries that had marked the separate space and distinct territories of the rulers, the distances that had been established over the past to keep them apart'.[204] Such scenes conveyed the message that 'there was no space, no territory, that was not owned by or accessible to the people of a Free India, and the Government and its territory were now the people's'.[205] The departing governor, his wife and ADCs had to be 'smuggled out' from the rear entrance, thus marking a finale to the passing of British rule in Bengal and signifying an 'incident free' coming of Independence to the city.

From Euphoria to Aporia

As the celebrations drew to a close it was ironic that 'national leaders' in their speeches during the official ceremonies were indulging in hollow sentimentalism about the minorities which had been left across the borders. For instance, Nehru declared with some emotion in his Independence Day message:

We think also of our brothers and sisters who have been cut off from us by physical boundaries and who unhappily cannot share at present in the freedom that has come. They are of us and will remain of us whatever may happen, and we shall be sharers in their good and ill fortune alike.[206]

Jinnah expressed similar emotions in Karachi for the millions of Muslims who were to find themselves in Indian territories once the Boundary Commission award became known. To them he offered these words of solace: 'Those of our brethren who are minorities in Hindustan may rest assured that we shall never neglect or forget them. . . . I recognize that it is the Muslim minority provinces in this sub-continent who were the pioneers and carried the banner aloft for the achievement of our cherished goal of Pakistan.' He advised them to 'adjust themselves to new and difficult circumstances' particularly because 'they might face resentment from the majority community for having supported the demand for Pakistan'. He counselled them to 'give unflinching loyalty to the state in which they happened to be'.[207]

Other leaders carried such tokenism even further. Vallabhbhai Patel, India's newly appointed deputy prime minister, in his Independence Day broadcast said: 'Our hearts go out to those who were with us so long but who are now to be separated. . . . Few can realise the bitterness and sorrow which partition has brought to those who cherished unity but lived to fashion its details'. He avowed: 'Let our brethren across the border not feel that they are neglected or forgotten. Their welfare will claim our vigilance and we shall follow with abiding interest their future in full hope and confidence that sooner than later we shall again be united in common allegiance to our country.' Likewise, on Independence Day morning, Prasad declared in the Constituent Assembly:

> It is undoubtedly a day of rejoicing. But there is only one thought which mars and detracts from the fullness of this happy event. India, which was made by God and Nature to be one, which culture and tradition and history of millenniums have made one, is divided today and many there are on the other side of the boundary who would much rather be on this side. To them we send a word of cheer and assurance and ask them not to give way to panic or despair but to live with faith and courage in peace with their neighbours and fulfil the duties of loyal citizenship and thus win their rightful place. . . . We feel assured that they all will be treated fairly and justly without any distinction or discrimination. Let us hope and pray that the day will come when even those who have insisted upon and brought about this division will realise India's essential oneness and we shall, be united once again. . . . It may appear to be a dream but it is no more fantastic a dream than that of those who wanted a division and may well be, realised even sooner than we dare hope for today.[208]

However, the attempt of the new rulers of India and Pakistan to baptise people into becoming citizens of the new nations was a colossal failure, as later events showed so dramatically. The political inheritors of the British Raj had been preoccupied with carving out territory for their respective nation-states. Their sole concern in the run up to the events of 14–17 August had been how to maximize their advantage in terms of political boundaries. It was extraordinary that in the protracted negotiations which took place among the British, the Congress and the Muslim League, there was a conspicuous lack of concern with the fundamental issue of citizenship. Questions such as what the creation of the new states would mean for the minority communities, their right of residence, and their status in the new nations were not even considered.

Following the outbreak of large-scale disturbances in the Punjab, the violence which erupted there and in other parts of the subcontinent was portrayed as 'religious strife', rather than as an assertion by the people of their right of residence, or an affirmation on their part of their natural citizenship to a land where they had been born or raised. In the event, the outcome was unprecedented violence and mass displacement. This has been poignantly but aptly summarized by Shorish Kashmiri, a poet, journalist and someone who was displaced as a consequence of Partition. He offers the following verdict on the events of 14–17 August 1947:

> Conches were blown in India. Drums were beaten in Pakistan. All India Radio proclaimed Independence by broadcasting Bande Mataram and Pakistan Radio did so with recitation of the Quran. But as day dawned, both sides began to butcher their minorities in the name of religion. . . . In India it was the Muslims who were butchered: in Pakistan the Sikhs and Hindus. Now the riots ceased to be communal. On the contrary, it was genocide of the minorities by the majorities.[209]

Several useful insights emerge from a reconstruction, however partial and imperfect, of the events of 14–17 August 1947. First, it is striking that responses to the celebrations were not uniform across the subcontinent.

There were distinct ways in which different cities and towns responded to the events. Such differentiation had everything to do with the location of the place itself in the larger territorial reconfigurations which were then underway. Second, the diversity of responses was also due to what Edward Shils has called 'cultural centres' and 'peripheries'.[210] Thus, the ceremonials in Karachi and New Delhi, which embodied self-constituted 'cultural centres' of core national values, played an important part in inviting participation and confirmation on the part of their 'peripheries'.[211]

Quite clearly, as the discussion has tried to show, cities like Delhi and Karachi were in the forefront of the commemorations, while others like Dhaka were 'backwaters' which had to be integrated into the process of national affirmation. At many places participation in the events was thin or sporadic. In the Punjab, all available evidence seems to suggest a complete absence of festivity, with mere ritual observances involving the salutation of flags and oath-taking by leaders. State rituals in that region failed to rally the people into participating in ceremonies which could bring them together into a community—imagined or otherwise—even temporarily.

Upon closer scrutiny it is quite clear that the imagery of rapturous popular expressions of joy across India and Pakistan at the coming of freedom seems no more than a larger than life, blown-up myth. The events of 14–17 August 1947 failed to create a sense of cohesion or consensus among different groups by bringing them together in a common celebration of the birth of the 'nation'.[212] Rather, the consecration rituals which the two nation-states staged with much fanfare and ceremony conveyed a range of diverse meanings to different groups. As this discussion has attempted to highlight, the rituals of Independence—as these were experienced by people at that time—had profound ambiguities. However, these uncertainties have either been effaced due to the passage of time, or new meanings have been invested to the events by state rituals which, through annual reiteration, commemorate only one aspect of the event—the birth of the nation.[213] As a consequence, the multiple meanings and the range of experiences of what the coming of Independence signified to people in India and Pakistan have been lost, if not significantly altered.

It is noteworthy that a few days before Independence, Gandhi expressed his sense of foreboding and aporia about the approaching event. He likened it to one of the mythical churning of the ocean from which the universe was created, according to Hindu beliefs. The *Harijan* in its 10 August 1947 issue noted:

> In the mythological churning of the ocean were discovered poison and nectar along with other valuable gifts. All the gifts were shared by the Devas and the Asuras. The Lord Shiva had to swallow the poison to save the world. The mighty struggle for India's independence might well be compared with the churning of the ocean. It has yielded the nectar of independence and the poison of partition. There are many who have had to swallow the poison of partition. Let us hope like the figurative Lord Shiva they will emerge all the stronger for the deadly drink.[214]

Clearly then, the effects of the events of 14–17 August 1947 were many and long lasting. A metaphor for these is provided by Salman Rushdie: 'Midnight has many children; the offsprings of Independence were not all human. Violence, corruption, poverty, generals, chaos, greed and pepperpots. . . . I had to go into exile to learn that the children of midnight were more varied than even I had dreamed.'[215]

Notes

1. B. Chandra et al., *India's Struggle for Independence*, Delhi, 1988; and R. Jeffrey, ed., *Asia: The Winning of Independence*, London, 1981.
2. R. Kumar, *Essays in the Social History of Modern India*, Calcutta, 1983, p. 1. Professor Kumar regards it as 'a stupendous achievement which opened the possibility of transforming the human condition within the country'. See his 'Partition Historiography: Some Reflections', in *India's Partition: Prelude and Legacies*, ed. Ramakant and R. Mahajan, Jaipur, 1998, p. 52.
3. The historian Jim Masselos has done interesting work on nationalist and state rituals. See J. Masselos, 'The Magic Touch of Being Free', in *India: Creating a Modern Nation*, ed. J. Masselos, New Delhi, 1988. While the stimulus provided by his work is gratefully acknowledged, the issues raised in this chapter and the argument canvassed here are quite different. Also see his 'India's Republic Day: The Other 26 January', *South Asia*, vol. 19, Special Issue, 1996, pp. 1–14.
4. For an interesting study of political ritual in another context, see L. Kong and B.S.A. Yeoh, 'The Construction of National Identity through the Production of Ritual

and Spectacle: An Analysis of National Day Parades in Singapore', *Political Geography*, vol. 16, no. 3, 1997, pp. 213–39.

5. For a run-up to the event based on newspaper reports, by a BBC radio journalist, see M. Upadhyay, *50 Days to Freedom: A Reconstruction*, Delhi: BBC, 1997.
6. Viceroy's Personal Report, 18 July 1947 in N. Mansergh, ed., *Constitutional Relations between Britain and India: The Transfer of Power, 1942–47* (henceforth *TP*), vol. 12, London, 1983, p. 230.
7. Cabinet, India and Burma Committee, Paper I.B. (47) 147, Ceremonies in India on 15th August and Flag, Memorandum by Secretary of State for India, 26 July 1947, L/P&J/10/136., in *TP*, vol. 12, pp. 62–3. The manner in which the flag at the Residency in Lucknow was removed and the precautions which the British took to ensure its safety is recounted in detail in Sir Francis Tuker, *While Memory Serves*, Delhi, 1950.
8. CRO to Dominion High Commissioners, 1 August 1947, in *TP*, vol. 12, p. 466.
9. Cabinet, India and Burma Committee, Paper I.B. (47), 43rd Meeting, Ceremonies in India on 15 August and Flag, Minutes, 28 July 1947, R/30/1/12, in ibid., pp. 381–2.
10. I. Copland, 'The Integration of Princely States: A "Bloodless Revolution"?', *South Asia*, vol. 18, Special Issue, 1995.
11. Viceroy's Personal Report, 8 August 1947, in *TP*, vol. 12, p. 595.
12. Viceroy's Personal Report, 8 August 1947, in ibid., p. 594.
13. Record of Interview between Mountbatten and Jinnah, 12 July 1947, in ibid., p. 122.

14. Interview between Ismay and Jinnah, 24 July 1947, in ibid., pp. 323–4.
15. Viceroy's Personal Report, 18 July 1947, in ibid., p. 231.
16. Interview, Mountbatten-Jinnah, 15 July 1947, in ibid., p. 164.
17. Viceroy's Personal Report, 18 July 1947, in ibid., p. 231.
18. The Constituent Assembly met for the first time in New Delhi on 9 December 1946 in the Constitution Hall, which is now known as the Central Hall of Parliament House. It was boycotted by the Muslim League and its first three sessions, which took place in December 1946 and January and April 1947, respectively, were held amidst controversy about its representative character in view of the boycott.
19. Cited in R. Grant Irving, *Indian Summer: Lutyens, Baker, and Imperial Delhi*, New Haven, 1981, p. 295.
20. Ibid., p. 295.
21. Ibid., p. 311.
22. *Hindustan Times*, 21 July 1947.
23. AICC Papers, G-8 (KWI)/1947–8.
24. Ibid.
25. *Hindustan Times*, 22 July 1947.
26. Shankarrao Deo, General Secretary, to all PCCs, 21 July 1947, Circular no. 28 (a), AICC Papers, G-8 (KW-I)/1947/8.
27. Lalta Prasad Saksena, Lecturer, Agra College, Agra, to Acharya Kripalani, 13 August 1947, AICC Papers, G-19, 1947–8.
28. Chhajju Singh, Secretary, District Congress Committee, Muzaffarnagar, to G.B. Pant, Premier, United Provinces Government, Lucknow, 16 July 1947, AICC Papers, G-19, 1947–8.

29. Mangla Prasad, Secretary, UPPCC, Lucknow, to all District, City and Town CCs, 30 July 1947. Source: AICC Papers, G-19, 1947–8.
30. Ibid., emphasis added.
31. Ibid.
32. *Dawn*, 3 August 1947.
33. *Dawn*, 28 July 1947.
34. *Dawn*, 6 August 1947.
35. First published in Nagpur in 1923 and reprinted in Bombay in 1969.
36. In the words of Christophe Jaffrelot, 'the Hindutva of Savarkar was conceived primarily as an ethnic community possessing a territory and sharing the same racial and cultural characteristics, three attributes which stemmed from the mythical reconstruction of the Vedic Golden Age'. C. Jaffrelot, *The Hindu Nationalist Movement in India*, New Delhi, 1993, pp. 26–7.
37. Jaffrelot writes that 'for Savarkar the territory of India cannot be dissociated from Hindu culture and the Hindu people'. 'In his eyes, Hindus are pre-eminently the descendants of the "intrepid Aryans [who] made it [the subcontinent] their home and lighted their first fire on the banks of the . . . Indus", a river which he considers to be the western border of the Hindu nation'.
38. Jaffrelot, *The Hindu Nationalist Movement in India*, pp. 26–7.
39. According to Bruce Graham, in 1947 the Congress

    contained within its ranks representatives of three important intellectual groups with quite different but divergent views of what form the new polity should take. Of these the first wished to see India as a liberal-democratic state with a constitution that was both secular and parliamentary in character; the second hoped for the formation of a socialist state in which collectivist principles governed social and economic organization; and the third was working to realize a state which embodied Hindu traditions and values. Each of these groups exerted considerable influence within the Congress and yet none was fully enclosed within it. For each one was generating its own distinctive pressure groups outside Congress boundaries.

See B. Graham, *Hindu Nationalism and Indian Politics*, Cambridge, 1993, p. 4.

40. See, for instance, J. Chatterji, *Bengal Divided: Hindu Communalism and Partition, 1932– 1947*, Cambridge, 1994.
41. At the end of 1947, RSS cadres of *swayamsevaks* stood at 600,000. The largest concentrations were in Uttar Pradesh (200,000), greater Punjab (including Delhi and Himachal) (125,000), Bombay (60,000), Bihar (50,000), and Punjab where numbers had risen from 46,000 in January 1947 to 59,200 by June 1947; see Jaffrelot, *The Hindu Nationalist Movement in India*, pp. 26–7.
42. D. Keer, *Veer Savarkar*, Bombay, 1966.
43. Vishwa Nath Singh to J.B. Kripalani, 16 July 1947, AICC Papers, G-19, 1947–8.
44. *Dawn*, 11 August 1947.
45. The Hindu right-wing activists disrupted the convention of the Hindi Sahitya Sammelan, held at Diwan Hall in Delhi on Sunday. They shouted anti-Congress slogans, broke the microphone and prevented Congress leaders from speaking. The convention ended in disorder. It was presided over by Pandit Balkrishna Sharma and prominent delegates included Pandit Ravi Sankar Shukla, Premier of the CP, Purshottanmdas Tandon, Speaker of the Uttar Pradesh Assembly, and Govind Malaviya, a member of the Consitutent Assembly.

46. Vishwa Nath Singh to J.B. Kripalani, 16 July 1947, AICC Papers, G-19, 1947–8.
47. There existed the 'need for rejuvenating our ideals in these turbulent times in the light of our religion and traditions', observed Adwait Kumar Goswami of Brindaban in a letter to Kripalani on the significance of the approaching event. 'Only religion can be the source of our eternal inspiration and religion must not be divorced from politics but should be its beacon'; he urged pressing his case to get India to declare itself a 'Hindu nation'. Adwait Kumar Goswami, Brindaban, 15 August 1947, to J.B. Kripalani, AICC Papers, G-19, 1947–8.
48. Hanumanprasad Poddar, Gita Press, Gorakhpur, to J.B. Kripalani, 5 August 1947 and his reply dated 19 August 1947, AICC Papers, G-19, 1947–8.
49. The conference was inaugurated by the Maharaja of Bharatpur, and attended by Sir Datar Singh, Shibban Lal Saxsena, Congress leader from eastern Uttar Pradesh and Seth Ramakrishna Dalmia. *Hindustan Times*, 9 August 1947.
50. 'Gandhiji's Speeches', *Harijan*, 25 July 1947.
51. Reported in *Hindustan Times,* 22 July 1947.
52. Ibid.
53. Interview with Begum Aizaz Rasul, Lucknow, 1989. Also see her statement in *Star of India*, 12 August 1947.
54. *Star of India,* 24 July 1947.
55. On this controversy, see *Hindustan Times*, 8–12 August 1947.
56. For details of Periyar's life and career, see A.R. Venkatachalapathy, 'Periyar E.V. Ramasamy', in *Oxford Research Encyclopaedia of Asian History*, see https://oxfordre.com/asianhistory/view/10.1093/acrefore/9780190277727.001.0001/acrefore-

9780190277727-e-340?rskey=pXFQXI&result=1, accessed 23 September 2022.
57. R. Kannan, *Anna: The Life and Times of C. N. Annadurai*, New Delhi: Penguin, 2010, p. 114.
58. M.S.S. Pandian, '"Denationalising" the Past: "Nation" in EV Ramasamy's Political Discourse', *Economic and Political Weekly*, 1993, pp. 2282–7.
59. Cited in Kannan, *Anna,* p. 116.
60. 'Tamil Nadu on August 15, 1947: Euphoria and Boycott', *Times of India*, 16 August 2016.
61. The Radcliffe Commission gave Sylhet to East Pakistan, except for Karimganj subdivision and three *thanas*, which were awarded to India. See https://partitionstudiesquarterly.org/, accessed 4 August 2022.
62. For a discussion of these issues, see Bertil Lintner, *Land of Jade: A Journey from India through Northern Burma to China*, Bangkok: Orchid Press, 2011.
63. Peter Steyn, *Zapu Phizo, Voice of the Nagas*, London: Routledge, 2006.
64. Diaries of Mildred Archer at the Naga Project, see http://himalaya.socanth.cam.ac.uk/collections/naga/coll/81/records/detail/all/index.html, accessed 4 August 2022. Also see Jelle J.P. Wouters, 'Difficult Decolonization: Debates, Divisions, and Deaths within the Naga Uprising, 1944–1963', *Journal of North East India Studies*, vol. 9, no. 1, 2019, pp. 1–28.
65. Sanjib Baruah, *In the Name of the Nation: India and Its Northeast*, Stanford: Stanford University Press, 2021, p. 102.
66. V.K. Nuh and Wetshokhrolo Lasuh, *The Naga Chronicle*, Indian Council of Social Science Research, North Eastern Regional Centre, New Delhi: Regency Publications, 2002. Also see Arkotong Longkumer, 'Bible, Guns and Land: Sovereignty and Nationalism

amongst the Nagas of India', *Nations and Nationalism*, vol. 24, no. 4, 2018, pp. 1097–116.

67. Diaries of Mildred Archer at the Naga Project, 23 August 1947, see http://himalaya.socanth.cam.ac.uk/collections/naga/coll/81/records/detail/all/index.html, accessed 4 August 2022.
68. *Dawn*, 3 August 1947.
69. Ibid., 30 July 1947.
70. Ibid., 26 July 1947.
71. Ibid., 30 July 1947.
72. Ibid., 8 August 1947.
73. Ibid., 30 July 1947
74. Ibid., 5 August 1947.
75. *Statesman*, 9 August 1947.
76. *Dawn*, 8 August 1947.
77. S. Hamid, *Disastrous Twilight*, London, 1986, pp. 227–8.
78. *Dawn,* 11 August 1947.
79. C.M. Ali, *The Emergence of Pakistan*, Lahore, 1967, pp. 239–40.
80. S. Wolpert, *Jinnah of Pakistan*, New York, 1984, p. 301.
81. A. Cowasjee, 'The Great Betrayal', *Dawn*, 10 August 1997; Hector Bolitho, *Jinnah: Creator of Pakistan*, Pakistan: Oxford Unversity Press, 1953.
82. A. Ahmed, *Jinnah, Pakistan and Islamic Identity*, Delhi, 1997, pp. 173–6.
83. A. Jalal, 'Conjuring Pakistan: History as Official Imagining', *International Journal of Middle Eastern Studies*, vol. 27, 1995, pp. 73–89.
84. Hamid, *Disastrous Twilight*, p. 228.
85. *Dawn*, 11 August 1947.
86. Wilfred Russell was an important British businessmen who joined Killick Nixon and Company in Bombay

in 1935 and was elected to the Bombay Legislative Council in 1937. See his *Indian Summer*, Bombay, 1951, pp. 123–30.

87. Hamid, *Disastrous Twilight.*
88. As a prominent Congressmen and personal friend of Jawaharlal Nehru, his memories of Karachi came from earlier associations such as the historic Congress session of 1931 when he was the General Secretary.
89. S. Prakasa, *Pakistan: Birth and Early Days*, Meerut, 1965, p. 12.
90. Ibid.
91. S. Kashmiri, 'Humiliated and Harassed They Left', in *India Partitioned*, vol. 2, ed. M Hasan, Delhi, 2012, p. 166.
92. A. Campbell-Johnson, *Mission with Mountbatten*, New York, 1985, p. 135.
93. Ibid.
94. Russell, *Indian Summer.*
95. Cited in Ahmed, *Jinnah, Pakistan and Islamic Identity*, pp. 23–4.
96. Akbar Ahmed observes: 'Although a great king, he was
    far from an ideal Muslim ruler. His harem had 1000 wives, he drank, introduced *din-e-ilahi*, a hotchpotch of some of the established religions, with himself as a focal point, which made the *ulema* unhappy'. Ibid., p. 176.
97. Ibid.
98. Hamid, *Disastrous Twilight*, p. 229.
99. Ahmed, *Jinnah, Pakistan and Islamic Identity*, p. 186.
100. T. Royle, *The Last Days of the Raj*, London, 1989, p. 168.
101. Campbell-Johnson, *Mission with Mountbatten*, p. 155.

102. Ibid.
103. See Royle, *The Last Days of the Raj*, pp. 58–9.
104. Cited in ibid., pp. 172–3.
105. M.A. Dossa, 'Karachi Club: August 1947', *Dawn*, 14 August 1997.
106. Campbell-Johnson, *Mission with Mountbatten*, p. 156.
107. *Dawn*, 29 July 1947.
108. Ibid., 1 August 1947. Bawa Bachittar Singh, a prominent Sikh member, suggested that the corporation should organize a procession. Mrs Ansari called upon Hindus and Muslim residents of the city to 'meet each other with the same feelings of brotherly love as one Muslim shows towards another on the day of Id'. Dr Yudhvir Singh, junior vice president of the Municipal Committee, said that on that solemn day they shall have to remember the great responsibility that devolved on a free people as Indians 'have attained their freedom after undergoing the baptism of fire, blood and tears'. Singh claimed that 60 lakh people had suffered imprisonment for one to twenty years in His Majesty's prisons in the struggle for freedom. Thousands had sacrificed their lives in the cause. Many of them were hanged by the government of the day. Others had suffered penal servitude and died in prison.
109. *Dawn*, 3 August 1947.
110. For instance, see the appeal of Begum Noor-us-Sabah, Secretary of the Women's Muslim League, Delhi, in *Dawn*, 5 August 1947.
111. *Dawn*, 5 August 1947.
112. Ibid., 29 July 1947.
113. Rajmohan Gandhi, *Patel: A Life*, Ahmedabad: Navjivan Publishing House, 1991, pp. 421–2.

114. Ibid.
115. See *Hindustan Times*, 13 August 1947 on preparations for these ceremonies; see also *Statesman* 15 August 1947.
116. Syed Mahmud cited in I. Douglas, *Abul Kalam Azad: An Intellectual and Religious Biography*, Oxford, 1988, p. 28. Shorish Kashmiri (1914–75), a prominent Muslim journalist and editor of the journal *Chattan*, recalls the occasion in the following words:

> Abul Kalam Azad—which means literally master of oratory—was not himself. He had become someone else. His heart was pounding. In his subconscious, his eloquence had conceded defeat. All his joys seemed fictitious. His cheerful countenance was struck with sorrow. He was overcome by depression Abul Kalam Azad wept in solitude. Lakhs of Hindus in the country were rejoicing. With them a throng of Nationalist Muslims, indulging in hollow laughter. But the hearts of crores of Muslims were seized with fear at the approaching morrow about to dawn, with daggers drawn and knives aimed at them.

See Kashmiri, 'Humiliated and Harassed They Left', p. 155.

117. *Independence and After: A Collection of the More Important Speeches of Jawaharlal Nehru from September 1946 to May 1949,* New Delhi, 1949, pp. 3–4.
118. For a valuable textual analysis of the anthem and its symbolism, see T. Sarkar, 'Imagining Hindu Rashtra: The Hindu and the Muslim in Bankim Chandra's Writings', in *Making India Hindu*, ed. D. Ludden, Oxford, 2006, pp. 162–84.
119. *Constituent Assembly Debates, Official Report*, vol. 5, New Delhi, 1947, pp. 4–6.
120. C. Khaliquzzaman, *Pathway to Pakistan*, Pakistan, 1961, p. 395.

121. S. Gopal, *S. Radhakrishnan: A Biography*, Delhi: Oxford University Press, 1989, p. 189.
122. U. Butalia, 'Blood, India! The Golden Jubilee', *Granta*, vol. 57, Spring 1997, pp. 24–36.
123. 'India: Fifty Years of Independence', *National Geographic*, vol. 191, no. 5, May 1997, p. 56.
124. 'The Scars of Partition', *The Hindu Folio* (Special Supplement of *The Hindu*), August 1997, p. 16.
125. 'The creative flow should not be contained', in ibid., p. 25.
126. M.R. Anand, 'Pride, despair, hope…', in ibid., p. 10.
127. Cited in Royle, *The Last Days of the Raj*, p. 216.
128. Hamid, *Disastrous Twilight*, p. 231. Nawab Ismail Khan (1884–1958), son of Nawab Ishaq Khan, a prominent landlord and one of the leading lights of the Aligarh University, was a lawyer and politician, a member of the Legislative Council in the 1920s, and one of the most prominent leaders of the Muslim League in Uttar Pradesh.
129. Masselos, 'The Magic Touch of Being Free', p. 45.
130. *Selected Works of Jawaharlal Nehru*, 2nd edn., vol. 4, pp. 2–3.
131. Masselos, 'The Magic Touch of Being Free', pp. 45–6.
132. Letter to the Editor, *Dawn*, 12 August 1947.
133. Editorial, *Dawn*, 15 August 1947.
134. Khaliquzzaman, *Pathway to Pakistan*, p. 396.
135. Begum S.S. Ikramullah, *From Purdah to Parliament*, London, 1963, pp. 135–6.
136. Jaluan Fire Works Co., Yahiaganj, Lucknow, to Acharya Kripalani, President, AICC, 26 August 1947, AICC Papers, G-19, 1947–8.
137. For a discussion of the context of violence in the princely states of Alwar and Bharatpur during 1947, see I. Copland, The Further Shores of Partition:

Ethnic Cleansing in Rajasthan 1947', *Past and Present*, vol. 160, August 1998, pp. 203–39.

138. *Hindustan Times*, 13 August 1947.
139. *Dawn*, 7 August 1947.
140. *Bombay Chronicle*, 7 August 1947.
141. D.F. Karaka, *From Betrayal in India*, London, 1950, cited in Hasan, *India Partitioned*, vol. 2, pp. 246–8.
142. Although he went to Gowalia Tank from where the procession organized by the Congress was due to start, his thoughts were about his family in Panipat in East Punjab. There, the Muslim residents which numbered 25,000 out of the town of 35,000 (including his mother and sister), had been threatened with forcible eviction to Pakistan.
143. S.K. Patil, *My Years with Congress*, Bombay, 1991.
144. Masselos, 'The Magic Touch of Being Free', pp. 44–5.
145. *Hindustan Standard*, 24 July 1947.
146. Ibid., 23 July 1947.
147. Ibid., 2 August 1947.
148. Ibid., 4 August 1947.
149. *Star of India*, 6 August 1947.
150. Ibid., 9 August 1947.
151. *Hindustan Standard*, 6 August 1947.
152. Ibid., 7 August 1947.
153. Ibid., 11 August 1947.
154. Ibid., 17 August 1947.
155. Ibid., 17 August 1947.
156. Ibid., 18 August 1947.
157. *Star of India*, 20 August 1947.
158. For an insightful study of the powerful 'mother' symbolism in the context of Indian nationalism, see S. Bose, 'Nation as Mother: Representations and Contestations of "India" in Bengali Literature and Culture', in *Nationalism, Democracy and Development,*

State and Politics in India, ed. S. Bose and A. Jalal, Delhi, 1997.

159. Diana Eck in her study testifies to the popularity of the Bharat Mata Temple among pilgrims to Banaras. See her *Banaras: City of Light*, New Jersey, 1982.
160. *Leader*, 16 August 1947.
161. *Hindustan Times*, 16 August 1947.
162. See Tan and Kudaisya, *Aftermath of Partition in South Asia*, Chapter 3.
163. *Dawn*, 6 August 1947.
164. Ibid.
165. *Dawn*, 9 August 1947.
166. *Star of India*, 10 August 1947.
167. Ibid., 13 August 1947.
168. Ibid.
169. Ibid.
170. Ibid.
171. Ibid.
172. *Harijan*, 9 August 1947, p. 293. Also see R. Payne, *The Life and Death of Mahatma Gandhi*, London, 1971, p. 533.
173. Ibid., pp. 533–4.
174. Ibid.
175. Ibid., p. 534.
176. *Harijan*, 10 August 1947, pp. 293–4.
177. B. Parekh, *Gandhi*, Oxford, 1997, p. 20.
178. Ibid., p. 21.
179. Talk of Manu Gandhi, 1 June 1947, in *Collected Works of Mahatma Gandhi*, vol. 88, Ahmedabad, 1983, p. 52.
180. Ibid., p. 52
181. Parekh, *Gandhi*, p. 21.
182. Ibid.
183. See, for example, speeches at prayer meetings, 16 June

and 24 June 1947, in *Collected Works of Mahatma Gandhi*, vol. 88, p. 164 and 204, respectively.
184. Letter to Munnalal G. Shah, 11 June 1947, in ibid., p. 130.
185. Ibid., p. 341.
186. Speech at prayer meeting, 10 June 1947, in ibid., p. 125.
187. Interview with Arthur Moore, a former editor of the *Statesman*, 10 July 1947, in ibid., p. 311.
188. Payne, *Life and Death of Mahatma Gandhi*, New Delhi: Penguin, 2018, p. 532.
189. Rajmohan Gandhi, *The Good Boatman*, New Delhi: Penguin, 1995, p. 351.
190. M. Green, *Gandhi: Voice of a New Age Revolution*, New York, 1993, pp. 377–8.
191. *Collected Works of Mahatma Gandhi*, vol. 89, p. 43.
192. Charles O. Thomson, American Consul to Secretary of State, 27 August 1947, US State Department (Confidential) Papers on South Asia.
193. Payne, *Life and Death of Mahatma Gandhi*, p. 536.
194. See H.S. Polak and P. Lawrence, *Mahatma Gandhi*, London, 1949.
195. Speech at prayer meeting, 20 July 1947, in *Collected Works of Mahatma Gandhi*, vol. 8, p. 380.
196. *Harijan*, 10 August 1947.
197. Payne, *Life and Death of Mahatma Gandhi*, p. 537.
198. Gandhi, *The Good Boatman.*
199. *Harijan*, 18 August 1947.
200. Charles O. Thomson, American Consul to Secretary of State, 27 August 1947, US State Department (Confidential) Papers on South Asia.
201. Ibid.
202. Ibid.
203. Ibid.

204. Masselos, 'The Magic Touch of Being Free', p. 44.
205. Ibid.
206. J. Nehru, 'The Appointed Day: A Message to the Press from New Delhi, 15 August 1947', in *Independence and After*, p. 5.
207. Cited in Ali, *The Emergence of Pakistan*, p. 239.
208. *Constituent Assembly Debates, Official Report*, vol. 5, New Delhi, 1947, pp. 1–22.
209. Kashmiri, 'Humiliated and Harassed They Left', in Hasan, *India Partitioned,* vol. 2, p. 155.
210. E. Shils, *Center and Periphery: Essays in Macrosociology*, Chicago, 1975.
211. For a useful discussion of how these centre–periphery ties have played an important role in two other contexts of national commemorations, see L. Spillman, *Nation and Commemoration: Creating National Identities in the United Statesand Australia*, Cambridge, 1997.
212. For an interesting discussion of what such rituals of commemoration try to achieve, see A. Bennett, 'Introduction: National Times', in *Celebrating the Nation: A Critical Study of Australia's Bicentenary*, ed. A Bennett et al., St. Leonards, New South Wales, 1992.
213. For a discussion of some of these issues, see J.R. Gillis, 'Memory and Identity: The History of a Relationship', in *Commemorations: The Politics of National Identity*, ed. J.R. Gillis, New Jersey, 1997.
214. *Harijan*, 10 August 1947. 'Devas' and 'asuras' are Hindi terms for gods and demons, and Shiva is the principal Hindu deity associated with the creation and destruction of the universe.
215. S. Rushdie, *Midnight's Children*, London, 1981, p. 291.

Epilogue

On 17 August 1947 people across the subcontinent awaited with trepidation for the Radcliffe Boundary Commission Award. It turned out to be a day full of ironies and paradoxes. At 9.30 a.m. Governor General Mountbatten flew into Bombay's Santa Cruz airport to a 'spontaneous and tumultuous' welcome, accompanied by his wife Edwina and daughter Pamela.[1] Although their visit was described as 'private', the 'streets were packed with cheering crowds still infected with the spirit and enthusiasm of the Independence Day celebrations'.[2] From Santa Cruz the Mountbattens drove straight to Ballard Pier to bid farewell to the first consignment of British troops returning home after the transfer of power. Before the ship sailed, Mountbatten mounted an improvised rostrum to gather the embarking units of the Second Battalion, the Royal Norfolk Regiment and Royal Air Force (RAF) personnel to cluster around him and addressed them in an informal manner. He was accompanied by Field Marshall Claude Auchinleck and Lt. Gen. Reginald Savory, Adjutant General of the Forces. Maj. Gen. K.M. Cariappa read out a message on behalf of Prime Minister Jawaharlal Nehru. Bands played 'Auld Lang Syne' as over 5,000 cheering British troops, packing the decks of the 28,000 ton trooper *HMS Georgic* waved 'an affectionate farewell to India and to Lord Mountbatten'.[3] Later, the premier of Bombay, B.G. Kher, hosted a tea party for the Mountbattens at the Taj Mahal Hotel. 'Popular demonstration reached unbounded height of enthusiasm', so much so it was reported that 'police cordons were swept away by the crowds'.[4]

In contrast, in the Punjab, an entirely different reality confronted Jawaharlal Nehru and Liaquat Ali Khan, prime ministers of the newly independent dominions, as they visited Ambala to begin their joint tour of areas in the Punjab which had by now been engulfed by largescale rioting and violence.[5] They held a meeting at the Circuit House with senior military and civilian officers from East and West Punjab. In attendance were Sardar Baldev Singh, Indian Defence Minister; Sir Chandulal Trivedi, Governor of East Punjab; Dr Gopi Chandra Bhargava, Chief Minister of East Punjab; Sardar Swaran Singh, Home Minister of East Punjab; and senior police officials. From the Pakistan side were present Sir Francis Mudie, Governor of West Punjab; Khan of Mamdot, Chief Minister, West Punjab; Mir Mumtaz Daulatana, Minister; and Chaudhary Mohammad Ali, Secretary-General of the Federal Government in Karachi. Senior Home and Police department officials attended, as did Lt. Gen. Sir Arthur Smith, Deputy Supreme Commander (Army), and Maj. Gen. T. W. Rees, Commander of the Punjab

Boundary Force. Nehru and Liaquat Ali Khan later also conferred with the prominent Sikh leaders, Master Tara Singh and Giani Kartar Singh. From Ambala the two prime ministers proceeded to Lahore and then to Amritsar. Upon the conclusion of their joint tour, they issued a statement at Amritsar declaring: 'It was unanimously decided that every possible step must be taken to stop this orgy of violence, arson and crime in both East and West Punjab.'[6]

Undoubtedly, on 17 August 1947, the centre of attention across the subcontinent was New Delhi, where the much-awaited award of the Punjab and Bengal Boundary Commissions, presided by Sir Cyril Radcliffe, which would decide the fate of millions of people in the Punjab and Bengal, was to be made public. As the details of the award were divulged, they were prefaced by Radcliffe's statement that in the two commissions' deliberations, 'the divergence of opinion among my colleagues was so wide that an agreed solution of the boundary problem was not to be obtained'.[7] In these circumstances, Radcliffe stated, that all members of the two commissions 'assented to the conclusion that he must proceed to give his own decision'.[8]

Perhaps it may be worthwhile to consider how the Radcliffe Boundary Commission originated in the first place. The idea of two Boundary Commissions to territorially divide the Punjab and Bengal originated in Mountbatten's blueprint for the transfer of power, known as the 3 June 1947 Plan, which had conceded, in principle, the demand for Pakistan: the Muslim-majority provinces of Punjab and Bengal, in view of their large non-Muslim populations, were to be divided. Two commissions were to demarcate the boundaries, based on the religious composition of the population, irrigation and transport infrastructure, and 'other factors'. Further, Mountbatten almost unilaterally decided to speed up the timetable for the transfer of power and set 14–15 August 1947 as the dates for the British departure.[9] He also decided that one person should be appointed jointly chairman of both the Bengal and Punjab Boundary Commissions. He further laid down that the chairman would have a casting vote in case representatives of the Congress and the Muslim League did not agree on the recommendations relating to the demarcation of territory.[10]

The individual whose name surfaced to jointly chair the two boundary commissions was that of Sir Cyril Radcliffe, Vice-Chairman of the General Council of the English Bar. Educated at Haileybury College and Oxford, Radcliffe was called to the Bar in the Inner Temple in 1924. During the Second World War, he served in the Ministry of Information in London and became its director-general when the war ended.[11] In this capacity, Mountbatten got to know Radcliffe and had been 'struck by his ability' and was enthusiastic about the appointment. Radcliffe had another important virtue: he had 'never been east of Gibraltar',[12] had no connections with India or with Indian affairs and had absolutely no local knowledge of the areas he was to divide. Despite his evident lack of expertise on India and his inexperience in boundary-making, no one objected to Radcliffe's appointment. Perhaps the promise of his impartiality was valued above all other considerations.

Christopher Beaumont, an Indian Civil Service (ICS) officer, who had earlier served in the Punjab, was appointed as Radcliffe's private secretary and 'minder'.[13] Beaumont met Radcliffe in the air terminal beside London's Victoria Station. Worried as to how he would recognize his boss, Beaumont waited and, in the end, 'simply approached the most intelligent-looking man in the room'.[14] He initially found Radcliffe to be 'a rather arrogant man, very self-important, almost pompous, unemotional. I never heard him laugh very much'.[15] He was nonetheless impressed by Radcliffe's 'formidable mind' and that 'he was totally incorruptible'.[16]

Upon arrival in New Delhi in early July 1947 Radcliffe spent his initial two nights staying with the Mountbattens in Viceroy's House. Beaumont recalled: 'There were just four of us at meals. Mountbatten and Radcliffe did not get on well. They could not have been more different. Mountbatten had few literary tastes. Radcliffe, a Fellow of All Souls, was of outstanding intelligence and very quietly civilised. Lady Mountbatten, to her credit, adroitly kept the conversations on an even keel.'[17]

Mountbatten took pains to project an image of impartiality, especially from official influence, by carefully keeping personal contacts with Radcliffe to a minimum. He insisted that arrangements for Radcliffe's stay should not be made in Viceroy's House in New Delhi. Further, Mountbatten refused to entertain any petition related to the boundary question. However, these demonstrations of non-interference in the work of the Boundary Commissions did little to quell the rampant and 'obstinate belief that Radcliffe [would] award as HE [Mountbatten] dictates'.[18]

Thereafter, Radcliffe and Beaumont were moved into another house on the Viceregal estate, which had no air conditioning, and the extreme summer temperatures seemed to affect Radcliffe's health and temperament. Beaumont scoured the Delhi shops for wine and 'he managed to find some cases of Alsatian which seemed to cheer Radcliffe up as he started work'.[19] With a nucleus of staff made up of Beaumont and Rao Sahib V.D. Ayer, an Indian subordinate who was appointed as assistant secretary, Radcliffe began work.

A detachment from local conditions may have contributed to an air of impartiality for the challenging job that Radcliffe was about to undertake, but it was also a serious handicap. As the final arbiter of the manner in which Punjab and Bengal would be partitioned, an overwhelming responsibility was placed on Radcliffe.[20] The geographer Oskar Spate has pointed out that it was a task probably too great for one individual even if his expertise had lain in boundary-making rather than in constitutional law.[21] Not only was Radcliffe unfamiliar with boundary-making, he was totally unaccustomed to the complexities of the regions he was about to divide.[22] Nevertheless, he was aware of the immense difficulties of the tasks that awaited him. In his first meeting with Mountbatten in New Delhi on 8 July 1947, he candidly pointed out that, given the vastness of India and its multitudinous populations, it would take 'the most careful arbitrators years to decide on a boundary that would certainly cut across homes and populations'.[23]

He was evidently shocked when told that he had only five weeks to complete his work.[24]

Radcliffe's brief was to demarcate the boundaries of the two parts of the province on the basis of ascertaining contiguous majority areas of Muslims and non-Muslims, while also taking into account 'other factors'. However, it was not made clear if all these factors came into play, which factor would gain precedence over the other. Demarcating areas based on geography and communal majority was complicated enough; but the politicking that ensued made the task even more daunting. The complexity of the task was soon made evident by the memoranda and representations submitted by the interested parties, principally the Congress, the Muslim League and the Sikhs. Not only was there limited consensus on the principle of communal division of territories but also sharp differences existed on how this principle was to be implemented.[25] Each political party made maximum demands in their submission of cases to the Boundary Commission to secure 'enough territory to accommodate the population and sustain a viable economy'.[26] Further, the internal working of the two Boundary Commissions could not be free from communal bias, as its members, nominees of rival political parties, diverged sharply in their views.[27]

Beaumont's accounts dispel the view that Radcliffe was 'treated like a hermit while he was working on the partition lines'.[28] Radcliffe travelled to Shimla, Lahore and Calcutta, and in Delhi he had frequent visitors, which included Sir Walter Monckton, Constitutional Advisor to the Nizam of Hyderabad; Field Marshall

Claude Auchinleck, Chief of the Army Staff; and Sir Patrick Spens, the Chief Justice. [29]

Although Radcliffe's award had been finalized by 12 August 1947, Mountbatten manoeuvred to delay its announcement.[30] It was believed that Mountbatten did not want the boundary questions to sully the Independence celebrations that he would preside over in Karachi and Delhi.[31] More importantly, it was likely that having seen Radcliffe's demarcations, he developed cold feet as he realized that the newly created boundaries 'would cause anguish to many millions of people on one side or the other of the frontier, and [would be] unsatisfactory to both governments'.[32] He justified the delay by saying that, although 'there was considerable advantage in immediate publication so that the new boundaries could take effect from 15th August', it had also 'been obvious all along that the later we postponed publication, the less would the inevitable odium react upon the British'.[33] Many felt the uncertainty caused by the delay made the situation in the Punjab even worse. Even Auchinleck complained that it 'was having a most disturbing and harmful effect',[34] but Mountbatten persisted and eventually had his way.

On 16 August 1947, after the Independence Day celebrations had concluded in Karachi and New Delhi, Mountbatten presided over a briefing convened in New Delhi with the intention of revealing, for the first time, the contents of the Boundary Commission Award. In attendance were Nehru, Vallabhbhai Patel and Baldev Singh from the Indian side, and Liaquat Ali Khan, Fazlur Rahman, the newly appointed Home Minister of

Pakistan, and Chaudhary Mohammad Ali who flew in from Karachi. Also present were V.P. Menon, secretary of the newly-created Ministry of States, and V.F. Erskine-Crum, conference secretary to Mountbatten. At this meeting, reactions to the Boundary Award from the Indian and Pakistani leaders were sharp. Nehru frankly expressed his outrage over the award of the Chittagong Hill Tracts to East Pakistan and demanded arbitration and adjustment. In particular, he expressed his fear that 'the award of the Boundary Commission in the Punjab was likely to have a bad effect upon the Sikhs'.[35] Nehru by now had received alarming reports from Lahore, where on the night of 15 August 1947, Dera Sahib Gurudwara, where thousands of Sikhs had taken shelter, had been burnt down by rampaging mobs. Reports indicated that Hindus and Sikhs gathered in relief camps in large numbers were living without proper protection and rations.[36] He proposed that he and Liaquat Ali Khan should undertake a joint tour of Lahore and Amritsar the following day and this was readily agreed.

Unsurprisingly, the Pakistani leadership's reaction was equally disappointed by the details of the Boundary Commission Award divulged by Mountbatten. While Fazlur Rahman defended the allocation of the Chittagong Hill Tracts to East Pakistan, he disputed the allocation of Darjeeling and Jalpaiguri to India. Liaquat Ali Khan said that 'the award, as a whole, was unfair to Pakistan'.[37] In Karachi, the Boundary Commission evoked strong reactions from official Pakistani circles. Sardar Abdur Rab Nishtar, communications minister, said 'it is extremely unfair and unjust to Pakistan and is based on no principles. We believe it is the parting kick of the British'.[38] Ghazanfar Ali Khan, minister for agriculture, said 'the award is disgusting'.[39] I.I. Chundrigar, commerce minister, also vociferously expressed his disappointment and hinted that, in the light of the award, Pakistan may not remain in the Commonwealth.[40]

Thus, finally, on 17 August 1947, the Award was made public and newspaper reports gave details of the newly demarcated boundaries in the Punjab and Bengal. Many had expected that Radcliffe's award would establish a 'makeshift boundary' which the future governments of India and Pakistan would review in the light of additional criteria, including the wishes of the communities affected and mutually adjust the borders after a process of arbitration. As the historian Joya Chatterji has pointed out, the border was 'never intended to be anything other than a rough-and-ready improvisation'.[41]

The Award for Bengal 'followed no consistent criteria' and was regarded as equally 'unfavourable to both communities, although the Muslim loss was greater'.[42] Six times longer than the Punjab border, after the demarcation of Punjab, the award gave East Pakistan an area of 54,501 sq. mi. for a population (based on the 1941 census) of about 40 million, of which 11.40 million, or about 27 per cent, were non-Muslims. West Bengal was given an area of 28,000 sq. mi., with a population of 21.20 million, of which 5.30 million, or 29 per cent, were Muslims.[43] The Radcliffe award gave West Bengal 36.36 per cent of undivided Bengal's land to accommodate some 35.14

per cent of the people. A portion of Sylhet district from the neighbouring province of Assam was appended to East Bengal to bolster its overall land size. West Bengal became India's smallest and most overcrowded province, with a high degree of urban concentration around the Calcutta area, soon to be swollen by the tide of incoming refugees.[44] West Bengal also became a food-deficit area, its agriculture being qualitatively as well as quantitatively inferior to that of East Pakistan. Not unexpectedly, under the Radcliffe Award, Calcutta was left in India, which also benefitted by the inclusion of the whole of Murshidabad, parts of Jessore and Nadia districts and part of Sylhet, which were all fertile areas. By doing so, more than a million Muslims were left out of East Pakistan.[45] As if to balance this loss, the Radcliffe Award gave the southern part of Jalpaiguri and the whole of Khulna district to East Pakistan. While the former did cause disruption to the main highway, the loss of Khulna, a district of 'mainly ill-drained soils, extensive swamp, and impenetrable wet forests', was considered of little consequence for India.[46]

Within the Bengal region the Award created large pockets of minorities on either side of the border, with each state having an almost equal proportion of majorities to minorities. In the north, the new boundaries created 'three obtruding salient of Pakistani territory into the Indian side, causing major disruptions to roads and railways in West Bengal'.[47] Willem van Schendel has shown that one 'bizarre' consequence was the creation of 197 enclaves over a 100 km. belt in north Bengal, out of which 123 were distributed to India and 74 to Pakistan.

Much like Bengal, the boundary line that divided the Punjab followed no consistent principle and was as illogical as it was problematic. It 'wobbled from communal to economic to strategic factors, followed no natural dividing features such as rivers or mountain ranges, cut across villages, canal systems and communication lines'.[48] Radcliffe adopted the demographic principle but applied it inconsistently. In some cases, he included an entire district in Pakistan because it had a Muslim-majority population. All the Muslim-majority districts were allotted to Pakistan, with the exception of Lahore and Gurdaspur. The non-Muslim majority districts went to India.

However, in the cases of Lahore and Gurdaspur, Radcliffe applied the demographic principle at the sub-district level or *thana* level, allowing 'other factors' to overwrite the agreed rule of division based upon communal demography. Although the district of Lahore had a Muslim-majority population, the awarded boundary meandered and shorn parts of Muslim-majority *tehsils* were included in India, possibly to minimize disruptions to railway communications and water systems. On the other hand, the entire district of Amritsar, which only had a slight majority of non-Muslims (53.50 per cent), was allocated in its entirety to India, despite the fact that its northern *tehsil*, Ajnala, had a Muslim-majority population.[49]

Perhaps the most controversial aspect of the Radcliffe Award in the Punjab was the allotment of the major part of the Muslim-majority Gurdaspur district to India, believed to allow India access to Jammu and

Kashmir. However, it is likely that the Gurdaspur Award represented Radcliffe's arbitrary and inconsistent use of 'other factors'—irrigation, communications, strategic—to determine where the boundary would fall.

As it turned out, no one was fully satisfied with the borders. As indicated earlier, Pakistan felt especially hard hit by the Award, describing the newly established border as 'extremely unjust and unfair'.[50] The new boundary in the Punjab caught everyone, including the provincial administration, by surprise. Hundreds of thousands of people, especially in the central districts of the Punjab, suddenly found themselves on the wrong side of the border after 17 August 1947.[51] The magnitude of the displacements and disruptions caused by the new boundaries far exceeded all official and non-official expectations. An estimated 4.50 million Sikhs and Hindus were uprooted from their homes in West Punjab and migrated, under appalling conditions, to East Punjab, which became a part of India, while almost 5.50 million Muslims moved in the opposite direction under similar conditions.[52] The loss in property on both sides of the border was tremendous. Some estimates have indicated that the loss could have amounted to Rs.1.50 billion.

Thus, Radcliffe's Award of 17 August 1947 engendered conditions that led to the 'other face of independence'—violence and mayhem, uprooting and largescale migration and subsequently the prolonged challenges faced in refugee resettlement and rehabilitation. Seventy-five years on, the memories of the upheavals and sufferings experienced during the course of Partition have not faded. In their own ways, individuals, families and communities are still coming to terms with how millions of lives were cruelly upended by the violence and the forced uprooting that followed in the wake of the imposition of new, arbitrary borders in August 1947.

In recent years, several efforts within civil society have led to tangible outcomes aimed at collective remembrance of Partition. One such key effort is the 1947 Partition Archives which originated in the US due to the initiatives of members of the South Asian diaspora and aims to create an online archive of oral history. The archives work with volunteers based in India, Pakistan and Bangladesh as well as in the diaspora at large. Till date, the archives has helped preserve over 10,200 oral histories of survivors and witnesses of Partition. A strong motif running through the archives' work is reconciliation and building bridges across borders as well as creating awareness among the younger generation about the complex and ambivalent histories of Partition. It aims at 'documenting, preserving and sharing eyewitness accounts from all ethnic, religious and economic communities affected by the Partition of British India in 1947'.[53] Another commendable effort, once again primarily driven by the younger generation, is 'The Generation 1947 Project' of the Citizens Archive of India, which aims to record and archive personal stories of citizens who witnessed life in pre-independent India and in the subsequent decades of nation-building. The project seeks to preserve letters, newspapers, documents, family pictures and other memorabilia, besides oral testimonies.[54]

In the cities of Amritsar and Kolkata, citizens' initiatives have led to the successful conception and setting-up of Partition museums. In Amritsar an impressive Partition Museum, spread over 17,000 sq. ft., with seventeen thematic galleries, was inaugurated in the historic and strategically located in the precinct of the former Town Hall, not too far from the Golden Temple itself, an area which has been pedestrianized to act as a magnet for tourists and visitors.[55] Inaugurated in August 2017, the Partition Museum is largely autonomous in its work, though it is supported by the state government. In Calcutta, the Kolkata Partition Museum Project (KPMP) began with an online launch in August 2022 and plans of eventually having a physical museum precinct.[56] The KPMP is specific in its objective of comprehensively memorializing Partition and bring out the specificity of the Partition experience for the Bengal region. It also seeks to build cross-border bridges between West Bengal and Bangladesh, highlighting the shared language and literature, food, culture and performing arts, and hopes for collaboration in the area of shared heritage. In Delhi, the ruling government has drawn up plans by designating the historic Dara Shikoh Library in the Kashmere Gate area, at the northern edge of the Walled City to set-up a Partition Museum. By doing so the Delhi government hopes to acknowledge the significant contribution of Partition refugees to the making of contemporary Delhi. It seeks to collect, curate and display material objects to be collected from individuals and families who lived through Partition and made Delhi their home.[57] These objects could be locks and trunks, pre-Partition ration cards, land deeds, photographs, etc. Renovation and restoration works are underway and it is expected that Partition Museum in Delhi will be launched in the near future.

In contrast to the civil society efforts, which are characterized by remembrances of human loss and suffering, nostalgia and a spirit of reconciliation, the present ruling dispensation has chosen to commemorate the 75th anniversary of Partition by remembering the pains of division. On 14 August 2021, Prime Minister Narendra Modi used two tweets to designate 14 August as 'Partition Horrors Remembrance Day' (*Vibhajan Vibhishika Divas*):[58]

> Tweet 1: Partition's pains can never be forgotten. Millions of our sisters and brothers were displaced and many lost their lives due to mindless hate and violence. In memory of the struggles and sacrifices of our people, 14th August will be observed as Partition Horrors Remembrance Day.
>
> Tweet 2: May the #PartitionHorrorsRemembranceDay keep reminding us of the need to remove the poison of social divisions, disharmony and further strengthen the spirit of oneness, social harmony and human empowerment.[59]

As is well-recognized, Modi has a dominant presence in social media and, unsurprisingly, his campaign has received acceptance from his huge following. Several top leaders of the BJP endorsed this campaign. For example, Home Minister Amit Shah congratulated Modi 'for taking this sensitive decision'.[60] On the same day, the Ministry of Home Affairs issued a notification published in the government of India's official gazette:

2 THE GAZETTE OF INDIA : EXTRAORDINARY [PART I—SEC.1]

MINISTRY OF HOME AFFAIRS

(Public Section)

NOTIFICATION

New Delhi, the 14th August, 2021

F. No. 2/7/2021-Public.—Whereas People of India while celebrating "Azadi ka Amrit Mahotsav" salute those sons and daughters of our beloved motherland who had to sacrifice their lives during the partition of India;

And whereas, the Government of India has decided to declare 14th August as **Partition Horrors Remembrance Day** (विभाजन विभीषिका स्मृति दिवस) in remembrance of the people who lost their lives during the partition;

Therefore, the Government of India declares 14th August as **Partition Horrors Remembrance Day** (विभाजन विभीषिका स्मृति दिवस) to remind the present and future generations of Indians of the pain and suffering faced by the people of India during the partition.

RAKESH KUMAR SINGH, Jt. Secy.

Several government agencies have taken forward this initiative of Prime Minister Modi. On 5 August 2022, the Government University Grants Commission (UGC) issued a directive to all affiliated colleges and universities in India to hold exhibitions to observe the 'Partition Horrors Remembrance Day'. The UGC stated that the exhibitions have been 'envisaged to bring to light the agony, suffering and pain of millions of people who suffered during the Partition' and 'to remind the country of the largest displacement of human population in the last century, which claimed the lives of a large number of people'. The UGC directed that the text and visual content for the exhibitions must use the material curated centrally by the Indian Council of Historical Research (ICHR) and the Indira Gandhi National Centre for Arts (IGNCA).[61] The Government of India's Ministry of Culture also announced plans to hold commemorative exhibitions on 'Partition Horrors

Remembrance Day' at 5,000 locations across India, including schools, colleges and post offices. A series of silent marches across seventy-five refugee colonies were also held.[62]

Unsurprisingly, this framing evoked strong responses in India and overseas. For example, Shyam Saran, a distinguished former diplomat, wrote: 'Remembrance can be a prelude to healing from a tragedy, to foster a determination among people to never allow the tragedy to repeat itself, but it can also be used to reopen old wounds and reignite ugly passions.'[63] Senior columnist and commentator, Prem Shankar Jha, described the announcement as 'mystifying'. While acknowledging the need to remember Partition, he urged: 'I believe we do need to remember it, to remind ourselves not to repeat the mistakes of the past: not to allow, let alone participate in, a wilful destruction of the uniquely tolerant and syncretic fusion of religions that India created over three millennia of coexistence between existing and newly arrived peoples, ideas and beliefs.'[64]

In Pakistan, the Ministry of Foreign Affairs denounced the move as a 'political stunt' and regretted this one-sided invocation of the 'tragic events and mass migration that occurred in the wake of Independence in 1947'.[65] Several leading Pakistani political leaders also protested at this labelling. For example, Shehbaz Sharif, then chief minister of Punjab, tweeted that the move 'shows a mindset that is deeply xenophobic and consumed by hatred towards Pakistan'. [66]

Scholars, curators and archives professionals questioned the choice of the word 'horror', which they acknowledge was an intrinsic part of the Partition experience. Yet such an approach, in their view, makes the commemoration unidimensional. Further, they explain that other aspects of the Partition experience—such as hope, sacrifice and resilience displayed by the survivors to rebuild their lives from a scratch—have remained unacknowledged and these qualities need to be remembered and honoured. In this context a suggestion has also been put forth that, instead of the 'Partition Horrors Remembrance Day', which prioritizes victimhood, a better approach would be to work towards celebrating a 'South Asian Reconciliation Day'. An ideal day to mark this would be 17 August, the day the Radcliffe Boundary Award was officially announced and published.[67]

As the subcontinent approached the 75th anniversary of Partition and Independence, sentiments within civil society seem to favour a type of commemoration that does not indulge 'othering' and divisive polarization. Such commemoration must acknowledge the complex, ambivalent set of circumstances in which communities—Muslims, Hindus, Sikhs, Buddhists and others—found themselves in the difficult and trying circumstances in August 1947, not of their own making, but imposed arbitrarily from above. Further, such remembrances must move away from using labels of 'victims', 'culprits' and 'perpetrators'. Further, they must acknowledge the loss of human life and trauma caused to individuals and families on both sides of the border and the efforts must be animated by a spirit of reconciliation that seeks to build bridges, renew the lost connectivity and reaffirm people-to-people contact in the years to come.

From the detailed account of the decisive days of 1947, described at length in this work, it is manifest that, if at all any day is to be commemorated as 'Partition Horrors Remembrance Day', it should be 17 August 1947—the day when the report of the Radcliffe Commission was announced which acted as a trigger for large-scale violence and uprooting of millions in the subcontinent. As is well known, 14 August 1947 marks not only the establishment of Pakistan, but also the late evening event when the Indian Constituent Assembly met in New Delhi in preparation for the Midnight Session where Jawaharlal Nehru delivered the 'Tryst with Destiny Speech' and members unanimously took the historic pledge of dedication to the new nation.

Notes

1. *Times of India*, 18 August 1947.
2. Ibid.
3. Ibid.
4. Ibid.
5. For the context of the unfolding violence in the Punjab and across north India, see Nisid Hajari, *Midnight's Furies: The Deadly Legacy of India's Partition*, Massachusetts: Houghton Mifflin Harcourt, 2015; Alex von Tunzelmann, *Indian Summer: The Secret History of the End of an Empire*, London: Macmillan, 2007; and Stanley A. Wolpert, *Shameful Flight: The Last Years of the British Empire in India*, Oxford: Oxford University Press, 2009.
6. 'Joint Action Statement to Subdue Violence', issued by the prime ministers of India and Pakistan, Amritsar, 18 August 1947, in A.S. Bhasin, *India-Pakistan Relations,*

1947–2007: A Documentary Study, vol. 1, New Delhi: Public Diplomacy Division, MEA, 2012, pp. 12–13.

7. *Times of India*, 18 August 1947.
8. Ibid. The Bengal Boundary Commission consisted of Justices C.C. Biswas, B.K. Mukherji, Abu Saleh Mohamed Akram and S.A. Rahman. The Punjab Commission members were Justices Mehr Chand Mahajan, Teja Singh, Din Mohamed and Muhammad Munir.
9. For a critical reassessment of Mountbatten's viceroyalty, see Wolpert, *Shameful Flight*.
10. This made the role of the chairman, with his casting vote, extremely critical. An earlier provision that the Punjab and Bengal commissions would elect their own chairmen was subsequently modified to provide for the appointment of a European chairman on the ground that it would expedite the work which had to be finished before the 15 August 1947 deadline set for the transfer of power.
11. For details of Radcliffe's career, see Edmund Heward, *The Great and the Good: A Life of Lord Radcliffe*, UK: Barry Rose, 1994.
12. Barney White-Spunner, *Partition: The Story of Indian Independence and the Creation of Pakistan in 1947*, UK: Simon and Schuster, 2017, p. 210.
13. Herbert Christopher Beaumont (1912–2002), Indian Civil Service, Punjab 1936–44, subsequently Indian Political Service 1944–7, Secretary to the Chairman, Boundary Commission, 1947.
14. White-Spunner, *Partition*, p. 210
15. Ibid.
16. Ibid.
17. Ibid., p. 211.

18. Major Short to Stafford Cripps, 3 August 1947, in *Constitutional Relations Between Britain and India: The Transfer of Power, 1942–47*, ed. N. Mansergh and E.W.R. Lumby, London: HMSO, 1970–83, vol. 11, p. 326.
19. White-Spunner, *Partition*, p. 210.
20. Following a subsequent amendment made to the Indian Independence Bill to the effect that 'the expression Award meant in relation to the Boundary Commission the decision of the Chairman of the Commission', Radcliffe was made singularly responsible for the boundaries that would divide India and Pakistan.
21. O.H.K. Spate, *On the Margins of History: From the Punjab to Fiji*, Canberra: National Centre for Development Studies, Research School of Pacific Studies, Australian National University, 1991, p. 53.
22. In recent years several studies have critiqued the boundary-making exercise in terms of its personnel, terms of reference, methodology of boundary-making, mode of working and, not the least, its time frame. See, for example, Lucy P. Chester, *Borders and Conflict in South Asia: The Radcliffe Boundary Commission and the Partition of Punjab*, Manchester: Manchester University Press, 2009; Hannah Fitzpatrick, 'The Space of the Courtroom and the Role of Geographical Evidence in the Punjab Boundary Commission Hearings, July 1947', *South Asia: Journal of South Asian Studies*, vol. 42, no. 1, 2019, pp. 188–207; and Tan Tai Yong and Gyanesh Kudaisya, *The Aftermath of Partition in South Asia*, London: Routledge, 2000, Ch. 3.
23. Leonard Mosley, *The Last Days of the British Raj*, London: Weidenfeld and Nicolson, 1961, p. 195.
24. Ibid.

25. Tan and Kudaisya, *The Aftermath of Partition*, p. 86.
26. Ibid., p. 201.
27. Joya Chatterji, 'The Fashioning of a Frontier: The Radcliffe Line and Bengal's Border Landscape, 1947–52', *Modern Asian Studies*, vol. 33, no. 1, 1999, pp. 193–5.
28. White-Spunner, *Partition*, p. 211.
29. Ibid.
30. The Radcliffe Award, in three separate reports relating to the Punjab, Bengal and Assam and Sylhet, is reproduced in full bearing the date of submission, 12 August 1947, in *Transfer of Power*, vol. XII, no. 488.
31. Alex von Tunzelmann provides a vivid account in her *Indian Summer*.
32. Ibid., p. 96.
33. *Transfer of Power*, vol. XII, no. 489, Viceroy's Personal Report, 16 August 1947.
34. Ibid.
35. JNSW, series 2, vol. 4, pp. 4–5.
36. For details of the unfolding violence in the Punjab and north India, see Hajari, *Midnight's Furies*.
37. 'Dissatisfaction with the Boundary Commission Award', *JNSW*, series 2, vol. 4, p. 4.
38. *Times of India*, 18 August 1947.
39. Ibid.
40. Ibid.
41. Chatterji, 'The Fashioning of a Frontier', p. 193.
42. Tan and Kudaisya, *Aftermath of Partition,* p. 94.
43. Ibid.
44. The effects of Partition in the Bengal region have been analysed at length by Joya Chatterji, *The Spoils of Partition: Bengal and India, 1947–1967*, Cambridge: Cambridge University Press, 2007 and Haimanti Roy,

Partitioned Lives: Migrants Refugees Citizens in India and Pakistan, 1947–1965, New Delhi: Oxford University Press, 2012.

45. Ibid.
46. Ibid.
47. Ibid., p. 100.
48. Ibid., p. 97.
49. Ibid., pp. 94–6.
50. Z.H. Zaidi, *Pakistan Pangs of Birth, 15 August–30 September 1947,* Quaid-I-Azam Mohammed Ali Jinnah Papers, Rawalpindi, 2001, p. 380.
51. For a discussion of these issues, see Ian Talbot and Gurharpal Singh, *The Partition of India*, Cambridge: Cambridge: Cambridge University Press, 2009 and Ian Talbot, *Divided Cities: Partition and its Aftermath in Lahore and Amritsar, 1947–1957*, Oxford: Oxford University Press, 2006.
52. Tan and Kudaisya, *Aftermath of Partition*, p. 98.
53. See alsp Neeti Nair, *Changing Homelands: Hindu Politics and the Partition of India*, Massachusetts: Harvard University Press, 2011. On the effects of Partition on border regimes, visa regulations and citizenship, see Yasmin Khan, *The Great Partition: The Making of India and Pakistan*, New Haven: Yale University Press, 2007 and V. F-Y. Zamindar, *The Long Partition and The Making of Modern South Asia: Refugees, Boundaries, Histories*, New York: Columbia University Press, 2007. '1947 Partition Archives', see https://www.1947partitionarchive.org/mission, accessed 4 August 2022.
54. 'The Citizens Archive of India', see https://citizensarchiveofindia.org/the-generation-1947-project/, accessed 4 August 2022.
55. 'Partition Museum Amritsar', see https://www.

partitionmuseum.org/about-us/#trustee, accessed 4 August 2022.

56. 'Kolkata Partition Museum Project', see https://kolkata-partition-museum.org/, accessed 4 August 2022.
57. *Hindustan Times*, 8 July 2022.
58. Ibid., 20 July 2022.
59. Twitter, @narendramodi, 14 August 2021, 1:07 PM.
60. Press Information Bureau, 14 August 2021.
61. Jagriti Chandra, 'UGC Writes to Colleges, Universities Urging Them to Observe Partition Horrors Remembrance Day', The *Hindu*, 10 August 2022, see https://www.thehindu.com/news/national/ugc-writes-to-colleges-universities-urging-them-to-observe-partition-horrors-remembrance-day/article65751030.ece, accessed 4 august 2022.
62. Damini Nath, 'Silent Marches to Recall Partition', Hindu, 9 August 2022, see https://www.thehindu.com/news/national/silent-marches-at-75-refugee-colonies-to-mark-first-partition-horrors-remembrance-day/article65750939.ece, accessed 4 August 2022.
63. The *Indian Express*, 19 August 2021.
64. Prem Shankar Jha, 'PM Modi, at the End of His Tether, is Intent on Wilful Destruction of Syncretism', The *Wire*, 24 Aug 2021, see https://thewire.in/politics/pm-modi-at-the-end-of-his-tether-is-naturally-intent-on-wilful-destruction-of-syncretism, accessed 2 August 2022.
65. *Dawn*, 14 August 2021; The *Express Tribune*, 14 August 2021.
66. Twitter, @CMShehbaz, 15 August 2021, 2:05 PM.
67. Debarshi Dasgupta, 'India PM Modi's Move to Remember Partition Trauma Stirs Old Wounds', *Straits*

Times, 18 August 2021, see https://www.straitstimes.com/asia/south-asia/partition-horrors-remembrance-day-divides-opinion-in-india, accessed 2 August 2022.

Glossary

Aatmanirbhar Bharat	self-reliant India
Akhand Bharat	indivisible India
Amrit kaal	term used by Narendra Modi to designate period from 75th anniversary of Indian Independence in 2022 to its centenary in 2047
Ashwamedh yagna	a Vedic ritual involving horse sacrifice
Azadi	independence
Azadi ka Amrit Mahotsav	literally, elixir of life; name given to 75th anniversary celebrations of Independence
Azad Pakistan Zindabad	Long Live Free Pakistan
Batwara	division; partition
Bhagwat Gita	Hindu ethical text
Bustee	habitation or neighbourhood

Darshan	literally, to view
dhams	abodes of gods
Dilli chalo	March to Delhi
Fateha prayers	Muslim thanks-giving prayers
Har Ghar Tiranga	Tricolour Atop Every Home
Havan	Hindu ritual involving fire-worship
Hindu raj	Hindu rule
Hindu-Muslim bhai bhai!	Hindus-Muslims are brothers!
Jai Hind	Victory to India or Long Live India
Jhandaabhivadan	salutation to the flag
Khadi	hand-spun cloth
Mahaparikrama	the great circumambulation or pilgrimage
Mahotsav	great festival
Mangaltilak	applying holy vermilion on forehead
Mazar	Muslim shrine
Om	one of the Hindu invocations to God
prayas	to strive
Quaid-e-Azam	supreme leader
Quaid-i-Azam Zindabad	'long livesupreme leader'
Raj	rule
shalwar	loose tapered trousers

sherwani	knee length buttoned up coat
Swaraj	self rule
Tarana-e-Hind	Iqbal's well-known anthem *Sare Jahan se achha*
tehsil	sub-district or revenue division
thana	police station
Tiranga	tricolour
Vibhajan	partition
Vibhajan Vibhishika Divas	Partition Horrors Remembrance Day
Yeh azadi jhooti hai, desh ki Janata bhookhi hai	This independence is a farce; the people of the country are still hungry!

Bibliography

Primary Sources

All India Congress Committee Papers, Nehru Memorial Museum & Library, New Delhi.

Cabinet, India and Burma Committee, Paper I.B. (47) 147, Home Department (L/P & J) Records, India Office Records, London.

Collected Works of Mahatma Gandhi, New Delhi: The Publications Division and Navajivan Press, 1978.

Constituent Assembly Debates, Official Report, vol. 5, New Delhi, 1947.

Constitutional Relations Between Britain and India: The Transfer of Power, 1942–47, ed. N. Mansergh and E.W.R. Lumby, vols 1–12, London: HMSO, 1970–83.

India-Pakistan Relations, 1947–2007: A Documentary Study, ed. A.S. Bhasin, New Delhi: Public Diplomacy Division, Ministry of External Affairs, 2012.

J. Nehru, *Independence and After: A Collection of the More Important Speeches of Jawaharlal Nehru from September 1946 to May 1949*, New Delhi: Publications Division, 1949.

Selected Correspondence of Sardar Patel, 1945–50, 1st edn., ed. Durga Das, Ahmedabad: Navajivan Publishing House, 1971

Selected Works of Jawaharlal Nehru, New Delhi: Jawaharlal Nehru Memorial Fund.

US State Department Confidential (Papers) on South Asia

Quaid-i-Azam Mohammed Ali Jinnah Papers, ed. Z.H. Zaidi, Karachi: Oxford University Press, 2001.

Newspapers

Bombay Chronicle
Dawn
Deccan Herald
Harijan
Hindustan Standard
Hindustan Times
Leader
Nation, Lahore
New York Times
Star of India
Hindu
Times of India
Tribune

Secondary Sources

Ahmed, A.S., *Jinnah, Pakistan and Islamic Identity: The Search for Saladin*, London: Routledge, 1997.

Ali, C.M., *The Emergence of Pakistan*, New York: Columbia University Press, 1967.

Ansari, S., *Life after Partition: Migration, Community and Strife in Sindh, 1947–1962*, Oxford: Oxford University Press, 2005.

Ansari, S. and W. Gould, *Boundaries of Belonging: Localities, Citizenship and Rights in India and Pakistan*, Cambridge: Cambridge University Press, 2019.

Bandyopadhyay, S., *Decolonization in South Asia: Meanings of Freedom in Post-independence West Bengal, 1947–52*, London: Routledge, 2009.

Baruah, S., *In the Name of the Nation: India and Its Northeast*, Stanford: Stanford University Press, 2021.

Baviskar, A. and M. Levien, 'Farmers' Protests in India: Introduction to the JPS Forum', *The Journal of Peasant Studies*, vol. 48, no. 7, 2021, pp. 1341–55.

Behl, N., 'India's Farmers' Protest: An Inclusive Vision of Indian Democracy', *American Political Science Review*, 2022, pp. 1–6.

Bennett, A. et al., eds., *Celebrating the Nation: A Critical Study of Australia's Bicentenary*, New South Wales: Allen and Unwin, 1992.

Bose, Sugata, 'Nation as Mother: Representations and Contestations of "India" in Bengali Literature and Culture', in *Nationalism, Democracy and Development: State and Politics in India*, ed. S. Bose and A. Jalal, Delhi: Oxford University Press, 1997.

______, 'Unity or Partition: Mahatma Gandhi's Last Stand, 1945–1948', in *Gandhi's Moral Politics*, ed. Naren Nanda, New Delhi: Routledge, 2017.

Butalia, U., 'Blood, India! The Golden Jubilee', *Granta*, vol. 57, Spring, 1997.

______, *The Other Side of Silence: Voices from the Partition of India*, North Carolina: Duke University Press, 2000.

Cannadine, David, 'Introduction: Independence Day Ceremonials in Historical Perspective', *The Round Table*, vol. 97, no. 398, 2008, pp. 649–65.

Campbell-Johnson, A., *Mission with Mountbatten*, London: Hamish Hamilton, 1985.

Chandra, B. et al., *India's Struggle for Independence*, Delhi: Viking, 1988.

Chatterji, J., *Bengal Divided: Hindu Communalism and Partition, 1932–1947*, Cambridge: Cambridge University Press, 1994.

———, 'The Fashioning of a Frontier: The Radcliffe Line and Bengal's Border Landscape, 1947–52', *Modern Asian Studies*, vol. 33, no. 1, 1999, pp. 185–242.

———, *The Spoils of Partition: Bengal and India, 1947–1967*, Cambridge: Cambridge University Press, 2007.

Chester, L.P., *Borders and Conflict in South Asia: The Radcliffe Boundary Commission and the Partition of Punjab*, Manchester: Manchester University Press, 2009.

Copland, I., 'The Integration of Princely States: A "Bloodless Revolution"?', *South Asia*, vol. 18, Special Issue, 1995, pp. 131–51.

———, 'The Further Shores of Partition: Ethnic Cleansing in Rajasthan, 1947', *Past and Present*, vol. 160, August 1998, pp. 203–39.

Cowasjee, A., 'The Great Betrayal', *Dawn*, 10 August 1997.

Dossa, M.A., 'Karachi Club: August 1947', *Dawn*, 14 August 1997.

Douglas, I., *Abul Kalam Azad: An Intellectual and Religious Biography*, Oxford: Oxford University Press, 1988.

Dubey, I., 'Remembering, Forgetting and Memorialising: 1947, 1971 and the State of Memory Studies in South Asia', *India Review*, vol. 20, no. 5, 2021, pp. 510–39.

Eck, D., *Banaras, City of Light*, New Jersey: Princeton University Press, 1983.

Fitzpatrick, Hannah, 'The Space of the Courtroom and the Role of Geographical Evidence in the Punjab Boundary Commission Hearings, July 1947', *South Asia: Journal of South Asian Studies*, vol. 42, no. 1, 2019, pp. 188 207.

———, 'Imagining and mapping the end of an empire: Oskar Spate and the partition of India and Pakistan', *Journal of Historical Geography*, vol. 66, 2019, pp. 55–68.

Gandhi, Rajmohan, *The Good Boatman: A Portrait of Gandhi*, New Delhi: Viking, 1995.

———, *Patel: A Life*, Ahmedabad: Navjivan Publishing House, 1991.

Gillis, J.R., 'Memory and Identity: The History of a Relationship', in *Commemorations: The Politics of National Identity*, ed. J.R. Gillis, New Jersey: Princeton University Press, 1997.

Gopal, S., *S. Radhakrishnan, A Biography*, Delhi: Oxford University Press, 1989.

Graham, B., *Hindu Nationalism and Indian Politics*, Cambridge: Cambridge University Press, 1993.

Green, M., *Gandhi: Voice of a New Age Revolution*, New York: Continuum, 1993.

Guha, R., *India After Gandhi: The History of the World's Largest Democracy*, London: Pan Macmillan, 2017.

Hajari, N., *Midnight's Furies: The Deadly Legacy of India's Partition*, Massachusetts: Houghton Mifflin Harcourt, 2015.

Hamid, S., *Disastrous Twilight: A Personal Record of the Partition of India*, London: Leo Cooper, 1986.

Hasan, M., ed., *India Partitioned: The Other Face of Freedom*, vol. 2, New Delhi: Rupa, 1995.

Heward, Edmund, *The Great and the Good: A Life of Lord Radcliffe*, UK: Barry Rose, 1994.

Holland, R., S. Williams, and T. Barringer, *The Iconography of Independence: 'Freedoms at Midnight'*, London: Routledge, 2010.

Ikramullah, S.S., *From Purdah to Parliament*, London: Cresset, 1963.

Irving, R.G., *Indian Summer: Lutyens, Baker and Imperial Delhi*, New Haven: Yale University Press, 1981.

Jaffrelot, C., *The Hindu Nationalist Movement in India*, New Delhi: Viking, 1993.

Jalal, A., 'Conjuring Pakistan: History as Official Imagining', *International Journal of Middle East Studies*, vol. 27, 1995.

———, *The Pity of Partition: Manto's Life, Times, and Work across the India-Pakistan Divide*, Princeton: Princeton University Press, 2013.

Jeffrey, Robin, *Asia: The Winning of Independence*, London: Macmillan, 1981.

Jha, S., 'Challenges in the History of Colours: The Case of Saffron', *The Indian Economic and Social History Review*, vol. 51, no. 2, 2014, pp. 199–229.

———, 'The Indian National Flag as a Site of Daily Plebiscite', *Economic and Political Weekly*, 2008, pp. 102–11.

———, *Reverence, Resistance and Politics of Seeing the Indian National Flag*, Cambridge: Cambridge University Press, 2015.

Kannan, R., *Anna: The Life and Times of C. N. Annadurai*, New Delhi: Penguin, 2010.

Kashmiri, S., 'Humiliated and Harassed They Left', in *India Partitioned*, vol. 2, ed. M. Hasan, New Delhi: Rupa, 1995.

Kaul, C., '"At the Stroke of the Midnight Hour": Lord Mountbatten and the British Media at Indian Independence', *The Round Table*, vol. 97, no. 398, 2008, pp. 677–93.

Keer, D., *Veer Savarkar*, Bombay: Popular Prakashan, 1966.

Kelly, D. and A. Reid, eds., *Asian Freedoms: The Idea of Freedom in East and Southeast Asia*, New York: Cambridge University Press, 1998.

Khaliquzzaman, C., *Pathway to Pakistan*, Lahore: Longmans, 1961.

Khan, Y., 'The Ending of an Empire: From Imagined Communities to Nation States in India and Pakistan', *The Round Table*, vol. 97, no. 398, 2008, pp. 695–704.

_____, *The Great Partition: The Making of India and Pakistan*, New Haven: Yale University Press, 2007.

Kong, L. and B. Yeoh, 'The Construction of National Identity through the Production of Ritual and Spectacle: An Analysis of National Day Parades in Singapore', *Political Geography*, vol. 16, no. 3, 1997.

Kumar, R., *Essays in the Social History of Modern India*, Delhi: Oxford University Press, 1983.

_____, 'Partition Historiography: Some Reflections', in *India's Partition: Prelude and Legacies*, ed. Ramakant Rajan Mahan, Jaipur: Rawat Publications, 1998.

Lal, Brij V., 'Of Ruptures and Recuperations: Fiji's Fifty Years of Independence', *Journal of Pacific History*, vol. 36, no. 2, 2021, pp. 185–97.

Lentz, Carola and David Lowe, *Remembering Independence*, London: Routledge, 2018.

Lintner, B., *Land of Jade: A Journey from India through Northern Burma to China*, Bangkok: White Orchid Press, 2011.

Longkumer, A., 'Bible, Guns and Land: Sovereignty and Nationalism amongst the Nagas of India', *Nations and Nationalism*, vol. 24, no. 4, 2018, pp. 1097–116.

Mahajan, S., *Independence and Partition: The Erosion of Colonial Power in India*, New Delhi: Sage Publications, 2000.

Masselos, Jim, 'The Magic Touch of Being Free', in *India: Creating a Modern Nation*, ed. J. Masselos, New Delhi: Sterling, 1990.

______, 'India's Republic Day: The Other 26 January', *South Asia*, vol. 19, Special Issue, 1996.

Mosley, L., *The Last Days of the British Raj*, London: Weidenfeld and Nicolson, 1961.

Nair, N., *Changing Homelands: Hindu Politics and the Partition of India*, Cambridge, MA: Harvard University Press, 2011.

Nayar, K., *Scoop*, New Delhi: HarperCollins, 2006.

Nuh, V K. and W. Lasuh, *The Naga Chronicle*, New Delhi: Regency Publications, 2002.

Pandey, G., *Remembering Partition: Violence, Nationalism, and History in India*, Cambridge: Cambridge University Press, 2001.

Pandian, M.S.S., '"Denationalising" the Past: "Nation" in EV Ramasamy's Political Discourse', *Economic and Political Weekly*, 1993, pp. 2282–7.

Parekh, B., *Gandhi: A Very Short Introduction*, New York: Oxford University Press, 1997.

Patil, S.K., *My Years with Congress*, Bombay: Prachure Prakashan Mandir, 1991.

Payne, R., *The Life and Death of Mahatma Gandhi*, New York: E.P. Dutton, 1969.

Polak, H.S. and P. Lawrence, *Mahatma Gandhi*, London: Odhams, 1949.

Prakasa, S., *Pakistan: Birth and Early Days*, Meerut: Meenakshi, 1965.

Radcliffe, C., *Not in Feather Beds: Some Collected Papers [by] the Viscount Radcliffe*, London: H. Hamilton, 1968.

Rajagopal, Arvind, *Politics after Television: Hindu Nationalism and the Reshaping of the Public in India*, Cambridge: Cambridge University Press, 2001.

Roy, A.G., *Memories and Postmemories of the Partition of India*, London and New York: Routledge, 2020.

Roy, Haimanti, *The Partition of India: A Short Introduction*, New Delhi: Oxford University Press, 2018.

———, *Partitioned Lives: Migrants Refugees Citizens in India and Pakistan, 1947–1965*, New Delhi: Oxford University Press, 2012.

Roy, S., '"A Symbol of Freedom": The Indian Flag and the Transformations of Nationalism, 1906–2002', *Journal of Asian Studies*, vol. 65, no. 3, 2006, pp. 495–527.

Royle, T., *The Last Days of the Raj*, Kent: Hodder and Stoughton, 1989.

Rushdie, S., *Midnight's Children*, New York: Random House, 1981.

Russell, W., *Indian Summer*, Bombay: Thacker, Spink and Co., 1951.

Saint, T.K., *Witnessing Partition: Memory, History, Fiction*, Delhi: Routledge, 2019.

Sangha, K.K., 'The Biggest Peaceful Protest against Corporations in Human History—Daring Farmers of India', *Journal of Agriculture and Ecology Research International*, vol. 22, no. 6, 2021.

Saran, S., ed., *India at 75: Aspirations, Ambitions and Approaches*, New Delhi: Observer Research Foundation, 2022.

Sarkar, T., 'Imagining Hindurashtra: The Hindu and the Muslims in Bankim Chandra's Writings', in *Making India Hindu*, ed. D. Ludden, Delhi: Oxford University Press, 1996.

Sen, U., *Citizen Refugee: Forging the Indian Nation after Partition*, Cambridge: Cambridge University Press, 2018.

Shils, E., *Center and Periphery: Essays in Macrosociology*, Chicago: University of Chicago Press, 1975.

Spate, O.H.K., *On the Margins of History: From the Punjab*

to Fiji, Canberra: National Centre for Development Studies, Research School of Pacific Studies, Australian National University, 1991.

Spillman, L., *Nation and Commemoration: Creating National Identities in the United States and Australia*, Cambridge: Cambridge University Press, 1997.

Steyn, P., *Zapu Phizo: Voice of the Nagas*, London: Routledge, 2006.

Talbot, Ian, *Divided Cities: Partition and its Aftermath in Lahore and Amritsar, 1947–1957*, Karachi: Oxford University Press, 2006.

——— and S. Gurharpal, *The Partition of India*, Cambridge: Cambridge University Press, 2009.

Tarlo, Emma, 'Khadi', in *Key Concepts in Modern Indian Studies*, ed. Rachel Dwyer and Gita-Dharampal-Frick et al., New York: New York University Press, 2015.

Tan, T.Y. and G. Kudaisya, *The Aftermath of Partition in South Asia*, London: Routledge, 2000.

Tuker, F., *While Memory Serves*, London: Cassell, 1950.

Upadhyay, M., *50 Days to Freedom: A Reconstruction*, Delhi: BBC, 1997.

Van Schendel, W., *The Bengal Borderland*, London: Anthem Press, 2004.

Venkatachalapathy, A.R., 'Periyar E. V. Ramasamy', *Oxford Research Encyclopedia of Asian History*, 2020, see https://oxfordre.com/asianhistory/view/10.1093/acrefore/9780190277727.001.0001/acrefore-9780190277727-e-340?rskey=pXFQXI&result=1, accessed 23 September 2022.

Virdee, P., *From the Ashes of 1947*, Cambridge: Cambridge University Press, 2018.

Virmani, A., 'National Symbols under Colonial Domination', *Past and Present*, vol. 164, 1999, pp. 169–97.

Von Tunzelmann, A., *Indian Summer: The Secret History of the End of an Empire*, London: Macmillan, 2007.

White-Spunner, B., *Partition: The Story of Indian Independence and The Creation of Pakistan in 1947*, New York: Simon and Schuster, 2017.

Wolpert, S., *Jinnah of Pakistan*, New York: Oxford University Press, 1984.

———, *Shameful Flight: The Last Years of the British Empire in India*, Oxford: Oxford University Press, 2009.

Wouters, J.J.P., 'Difficult Decolonization: Debates, Divisions, and Deaths within the Naga Uprising, 1944–1963', *Journal of North East India Studies*, vol. 9, no. 1, 2019, pp. 1–28.

Zamindar, V.F-Y., *The Long Partition and The Making of Modern South Asia: Refugees, Boundaries, Histories*, New York: Columbia University Press, 2007.

Internet Sources

'1947 Partition Archives', see https://www.1947partitionarchive.org/mission.

ANI, 'Amit Shah Calls upon People to Join "Har Ghar Tiranga" Programme', *The Print*, 2 August 2022, see https://theprint.in/india/amit-shah-calls-upon-people-to-join-har-ghar-tiranga-programme/1066407/, accessed 4 August 2022.

ANI, '"Azadi ka Amrit Mahotsav" Celebration: Centre to release Special Category Prisoners in Three Phases', *FirstPost*, 16 June 2022, see https://www.firstpost.com/india/azadi-ka-amrit-mahotsav-celebration-centre-to-release-special-category-prisoners-in-three-phases-10800871.html, accessed 4 August 2022.

ANI, 'Historic Chess Olympiad Torch Relay Covers over

20 Cities across India', *Asian News International*, 29 June 2022, see https://www.aninews.in/news/sports/others/historic-chess-olympiad-torch-relay-covers-over-20-cities-across-india20220629163219/, accessed 4 August 2022.

'Azadi Ka Amrit Mahotsav', see https://amritmahotsav.nic.in/index.htm.

Chandra, Jagriti, 'UGC Writes to Colleges, Universities Urging Them to Observe Partition Horrors Remembrance Day', Hindu, 10 August 2022, see https://www.thehindu.com/news/national/ugc-writes-to-colleges-universities-urging-them-to-observe-partition-horrors-remembrance-day/article65751030.ece, accessed, accessed 4 August 2022.

'Diaries of Mildred Archer, the Naga Project', see http://himalaya.socanth.cam.ac.uk/collections/naga/coll/81/records/detail/all/index.html.

Dakshina Murthy, K.S., 'After Indira Gandhi in 1973, India's Tryst with Second Time Capsule', *The Federal*, 28 July 2020, see https://thefederal.com/features/after-indira-gandhi-in-1973-indias-tryst-with-second-time-capsule/.

Dasgupta, Debarshi, 'India PM Modi's Move to Remember Partition Trauma Stirs Old Wounds', *Straits Times*, 18 August 2021, see https://www.straitstimes.com/asia/south-asia/partition-horrors-remembrance-day-divides-opinion-in-india, accessed 2 August 2022.

'HM Amit Shah Launches Doordarshan Serial—"Swaraj: Bharat ke Swatantrata Sangram ki Samagra Gatha"', *All India Radio News Service Division*, see https://newsonair.gov.in/News?title=Home-Minister-Amit-Shah-launches-serial-Swaraj---Bharat-Ke-Swatantrata-Sangram-ki-Samagra-Gatha%3B-Urges-youth-to-take-pride-in-country%26%2339%3Bs-history&id=445507, accessed 4 August 2022.

Joneja, Anisha, 'Union Budget 2022–3: What Does "Amrit Kaal" Mean?', *Deccan Herald*, 1 February 2022, see https://www.deccanherald.com/business/union-budget/union-budget-2022-23-what-does-amrit-kaal-mean-1076822.html, accessed 4 August 2022.

Jha, Prem Shankar, 'PM Modi, at the End of His Tether, is Intent on Wilful Destruction of Syncretism', *The Wire*, 24 August 2021, see https://thewire.in/politics/pm-modi-at-the-end-of-his-tether-is-naturally-intent-on-wilful-destruction-of-syncretism, accessed 2 August 2022

'Kolkata Partition Museum Project', see https://kolkata-partition-museum.org/.

Menon, Prakash, 'Har Ghar Tiranga is a Good Idea, but Not Every Indian Has the Means to Follow the Indian Flag Code', *The Print*, 2 August 2022, see https://theprint.in/opinion/har-ghar-tiranga-is-a-good-idea-but-not-every-indian-has-the-means-to-follow-flag-code/1064181/, accessed 4 August 2022.

Nath, Damini, 'Silent Marches to Recall Partition', The *Hindu*, 9 August 2022, see https://www.thehindu.com/news/national/silent-marches-at-75-refugee-colonies-to-mark-first-partition-horrors-remembrance-day/article65750939.ece, accessed 4 August 2022.

'Partition Museum Amritsar', see https://www.partition museum.org/about-us/#trustee.

Partition Studies Quarterly, see https://partitionstudies quarterly.org/.

PTI, 'PM Modi Launches New Series of Coins with Azadi ka Amrit Mahotsav Design', *Business Standard*, 6 June 2022, see https://www.business-standard.

com/article/current-affairs/pm-modi-launches-new-series-of-coins-with-azadi-ka-amrit-mahotsav-design-122060600752_1.html, accessed 4 August 2022.

Punwani, Jyoti, 'The Amended Flag Code: A Farewell to Khadi', *Deccan Herald*, 18 July 2022, see https://www.deccanherald.com/opinion/the-amended-flag-code-a-farewell-to-khadi-1127733.html, accessed 4 August 2022.

'Statista', see https://www.statista.com/statistics/827159/india-most-followed-twitter-accounts/.

'The Citizens Archive of India', https://citizensarchiveofindia.org/the-generation-1947-project/.

Index

Aatmanirbhar Bharat 1
Abbas, Khwaja Ahmad 111
Akhand Bharat 44
All India Hindu Convention 45
All India Hindu Mahasabha 43
All India Radio 53, 135
Alvi, Arif 1
Ambedkar, B.R. 5
Amrit Kaal 11, 13
Annadurai, C.N. 52
Archer, Mildred 54–5
Archer, W.G. 54
army 65, 76, 95, 155
Arya Samaj 95
astrology 11, 30
  dates of transfer of power 30–1
  Vedic astrology 11
Azadi Ka Amrit Mahotsav 1, 11–12
Azad Maidan 5
'*Azad Pakistan Zindabad*' 117

Beaumont, Christopher 158
Bengal Congress Committee 122
Bharat Mata Temple 119, 151n159
Bharatiya Janata Party (BJP) 169
Bolitho, Hector 63
Bombay 5, 24, 76–7, 108–12, 118, 145n86, 154–5
  Bombay Pradesh Congress Committee 108–9
  Bombay Provincial Muslim League 109
  Gateway of India 111
Bose, Subhas Chandra (also Netaji) 6, 12, 105
Boundary Commission(s) 53, 121, 133, 154, 156–8, 160–2
British/colonial army
  departure of 40, 54

Calcutta Muslim League 122–3
Cannadine, David 2

caste 61, 101, 110–11, 117
Chittagong Hill Tracts (CHT) 53
Christian community 43, 48, 77, 95
citizenship 2, 27, 85, 101, 113–5
Commonwealth 31, 163
Communist(s) 6, 79, 117, 130
Constituent Assembly (CA), of India 5, 30, 33, 92, 113, 134, 140n18
  crowd scenes 82, 91, 96
  midnight session 82–5, 88–91, 173
  oath of allegiance 91–2
corruption 9, 60, 138
Covid-19 pandemic 14
  post-Covid world 13
  public health crisis 14
cow protection 47

Damodaran, A.K. 92
Delhi 2, 6–7, 19n9, 26, 28–9, 33–5, 53–4, 64, 108, 120, 129, 136, 140n18, 156, 158–9, 161, 173
  Central Vista 81
  Chandni Chowk 95
  Delhi Bar Association 95
  Delhi Municipal Corporation (DMC) 78
  Delhi Muslim League 80
  Harijan Colony 35
  India Gate 7
  Red Fort 5, 7–8, 16, 35, 99, 101, 105–7
Deo, Shankarrao 36
Desai, Morarji 108
Dhaka 112–15, 117–18, 136
  Dhaka Congress Committee 113
Dilli Chalo! 15
'Direct Action' 120
Dravida boycott 50–3
Dravida Kazagham (DK) 51–2
Durbar Hall 31
  swearing-in ceremony 93
  Viceroy's House 92

East Bengal 50, 43–4, 60, 113–16, 120–2, 164
East Pakistan 53–4, 112–13, 144n61, 162–4

Father of the Nation 10
Flag Code 17–18, 22n41
flag-hoisting ceremony 9, 26, 36, 38, 94, 106, 109, 120, 131
founder(s)/founding father(s) 2, 26, 34, 68
freedom fighter(s) 5–6, 26

Gandhi, Mohandas Karamchand (also Mahatma Gandhi) 8, 10, 17, 31, 47–8, 51, 54, 83, 120, 123–31, 137
  fast against violence 129
  in Calcutta 120–5, 127–30
  Noakhali 120, 123–4
  opposition to Partition 31, 48–9, 125–7, 137

rights of minorities 49, 123–5
Gandhi, Indira 4–5
Gandhi, Rajmohan 81
Generation 1947 Project, The 167
Ghosh, Prafulla 130
Ghosh, S.M. 114
Gracey, Douglas 76
Great Calcutta Killings of 1946 49
Guha, Samar 6
Gupta, J.C. 115

Hamid, Shahid 65, 67, 74, 98
Har Ghar Tiranga 16
Haroon, Yusuf 57
Hidayatullah, Ghulam Hussain 76
Hindu Mahasabha 44, 79
Hindu–Muslim
  unity 120, 124, 129
  violence 107, 126
Hindu nationalist(s) 43–4, 47–8
Hindu *raj* 123
Hindu(s) 22n38, 38, 41, 43–50, 60–2, 65, 76–7, 79, 81–3, 106–7, 111–30, 135, 137, 141n37, 142n39, 143n47, 147n108, 148n118, 162, 166, 172
Hindutva 21n38, 43–4, 46, 141n36

Independence Day 8, 24, 48, 76, 105, 115, 121–2, 124, 128–9, 132–4
  boycott of celebrations 6, 44–6, 48, 50, 55, 79, 140n18, 129
  celebration/ceremony 2, 4, 18n6, 24, 26, 114, 121, 154, 161
Independence Day Celebration Committee 77
  plan(s) 1, 5–6, 10, 13, 27–31, 33, 35, 43, 45, 48, 50, 56–7, 79, 110, 114, 121–2
  swearing-in ceremony 31, 116
Indian Civil Service (ICS) 158
Indian national calendar
  new design for 37
Indian National Congress (also Congress) 3, 28, 30, 32–41, 43–7, 50–1, 54, 57, 60, 66, 78–80, 83, 100, 105, 108, 113–16, 118–24, 126, 135, 141n39, 142n45, 146n88, 150n142, 157, 160
  cadres 38–40, 94
  Congress Seva Dal 94
  Congress Working Committee 35–7, 50, 66, 108, 113, 115, 122, 126
Iqbal, Allama Mohammad 2, 9
Irving, Robert Grant 34

Jinnah, Muhammad Ali 2, 9–10, 25, 28, 31–2, 51, 57–60, 62–5, 67–78, 114, 117, 122, 125, 133

Karachi 2, 8–10, 28, 30, 41–3, 55–70, 72, 75, 77–8, 124,

133, 136, 147n105, 155, 161–2
Bohri Muslim/Dawoodi Bohra community 76, 109
Karachi Club 75
Karaka, D.F. 92
Kashi Utsav 12
Kaur, Rajkumari Amrit 83
khadi 17
Khaliquzzaman, Chaudhari 89–90, 107
Khan, Ashfaq Alam 105
Khan, Ayub 65
Khan, Gul Hassan 58
Khan, Ismail 98–9
Khan, Liaquat Ali 41, 50, 56, 155–6, 161–2
Khan, Zafar Ali 68
Khwaja Habibullah 115
Kolkata Partition Museum Project (KPMP) 168
Kripalani, J.B 37, 45–6, 50, 94, 143n37
Kripalani, Sucheta 83, 94

Lahore 8–9, 65, 127, 156, 160, 162, 165

Malkani, N.R. 57
Mehta, Hansa 91
Menon, V.P. 80
minority/minorities 41–2, 54, 60–1, 77, 90, 113, 115–17, 121, 123, 125, 132–3, 135, 164
concerns 25, 43, 49, 65, 80, 112–14, 117
rights 62, 71, 78, 84, 114, 116
safety 43, 122, 135
Modi, Narendra 10–11
Mountbatten, Edwina 30, 70, 92, 154, 158
Mountbatten, Louis 28–33, 66–7, 92, 94–5, 96, 98, 131, 154–9, 161–2
in Pakistan 28, 68, 70–2
Mukherjee, S.P. 114
Munshi, K.M. 44
Muslim League 28, 35, 38, 41
Muslim(s) 1, 9, 28, 32, 38, 40–1, 43, 45–6, 48–51, 54, 56–7, 60–2, 65–6, 71, 75–80, 82, 89, 98–9, 105–7, 109, 111–14, 117, 119, 121–30, 133, 135, 140n18, 146n96, 147n108, 156–7, 160, 163–6, 172

Naga declaration, of ‘independence’ 53–5
Naga Hills 54–5
Naga National Council 54–5
Namboodiripad, E.M S. 6
Narayanan, K.R. 8
national anthem 7, 9, 42
Jana Gana Mana 91
Pak sarzameen shad bad 42
national flag(s) 7, 38, 96
India 8, 16–17, 32, 38, 91–2, 94–6, 100, 106, 111, 115–16, 118, 109, 118–20, 122, 130

Pakistan 8, 41–2, 74, 115–16, 122
nationalism 62, 125–6
nationalist songs 85
Nehru, Jawaharlal 3, 8, 25, 30, 54, 83, 87–8, 90, 102, 146n88, 155, 173
non-Muslim communities 77
non-Muslim members
East Bengal Legislative Assembly 113
Pakistan Constituent Assembly 113
North-Western Frontier Province (NWFP) 50, 107

Pakistan
challenges as a new nation 4, 60–1, 68
as Islamic homeland 9, 77–8
as a secular state 61–3, 110
Pakistan Constituent Assembly 41–2, 59, 60, 62, 113
Pakistan Independence Day 115
Partition
anxieties over 25, 43, 49–50, 54, 65, 77, 80, 109, 112–13, 124–6, 128, 148n116, 162
opposition to Partition 31, 43
opposition to violence 123
minorities 25, 43, 49, 62, 65, 71, 78, 80, 84, 112–14, 116–17, 122, 124, 128, 135
safety of Muslims 79–80, 109
memories 25–6, 89, 91, 169
violence 25, 52, 78–9, 107, 120–1, 126–8, 135, 155–6, 166–7, 169, 173
Partition Archives 167
Partition Horrors Remembrance Day 169, 172–3
Patel, Vallabhbhai 80–2, 133, 161
Patil, S.K. 108
Phizo, Angami Zapu 54–5
Prasad, Rajendra 47, 81–3, 92–3, 134
Provincial Congress Committees 36
Punjab Boundary Force 65
Punjab Congress Committee 50

'Quit India' movement 79, 118
Radcliffe Award (also Boundary Commission Award) 133, 154, 156, 161–6, 172
Gurdaspur Award 166
Radcliffe Commission 53, 144n61, 156, 173. *See also* Boundary Commission
anticipated fears and anxiety 25, 154
composition 157, 173
delay in announcing award 161
details of award for Punjab and Bengal 156, 163–6
terms of reference 175n22
time-frame 157, 175n22
Radcliffe, Cyril 156–61
Radhakrishnan, Sarvepalli 81, 90, 94

Radio Pakistan 68
Ram, Mukhi Govind 57
Ramaswamy Naicker, E.V. (also 'Periyar') 51–2
Rashtriya Swayamsevak Sangh (RSS) 43–4, 142n41
Rasul, Begum Aizaz 49
ration(s)/rationing 108, 169
refugee(s) 63, 65, 107–8, 164, 166, 168, 171
riot(s) 107, 120, 131, 135, 155
river(s) 44, 119, 141n37, 165
Royal Air Force (RAF) 154
Roy, Kiron Shankar 60
Russell, Wilfred 64

Sabarmati Ashram 10
Santan Dharma Sabha 95
Savarkar, Vinayak Damodar 43–6, 141n36–7
Scheduled Castes' Federation 117
Sharif, Nawaz 8–9
Shils, Edward 136
Siddique, Sham Mohammed 106
Sikh(s) 43, 48, 50, 60, 65, 77, 107, 111, 135, 147n108, 156, 160, 162, 166, 172
Sind Minorities Association 41
Sind Muslim League 57
Suhrawardy, Huseyn 124, 128

Tandon, Purushottam Das 44
transfer of power 25, 28, 30, 33, 35, 42, 56, 64–5, 78, 154, 156–7, 174n10
'Tryst-with-Destiny' 8, 81, 85, 89, 173
'two-nation' theory 2, 62, 125
Tyagi, Mahavir 34

Vande Mataram 83, 89, 108, 110, 122

West Bengal 49, 113, 123, 130, 163–4, 168
women
  rights 51
  role in Independence Day celebrations 82, 91

Yusuf, Haji Seth Mohammed 49

www.ingramcontent.com/pod-product-compliance
Ingram Content Group UK Ltd.
Pitfield, Milton Keynes, MK11 3LW, UK
UKHW041644190726
13854UKWH00006B/2692